WALKS IN
LANCASHIRE WITCH COUNTRY

30 SHORT CIRCULAR WALKS
ON AND AROUND
PENDLE HILL

JACK KEIGHLEY

THE FAMOUS 'WITCHES' SHOP'
AT NEWCHURCH IN PENDLE

WALKS IN LANCASHIRE WITCH COUNTRY

an illustrated guide to thirty walks
on and around Pendle Hill

by

JKeighley

ISBN 1 85284 093 5

Also by *J Keighley*

WALKS IN THE YORKSHIRE DALES
ISBN 1 85284 034 X

**WALKS IN THE YORKSHIRE DALES
BOOK TWO**
ISBN 1 85284 065 X

**WALKS IN THE YORKSHIRE DALES
BOOK THREE**
ISBN 1 85284 085 4

INTRODUCTION

In 1612 ten 'Pendle Witches' went to the scaffold. These depraved wretches and their supposed victims lived in the villages and farmsteads surrounding Pendle Hill. Though nearly four centuries have since elapsed, the drama has never been forgotten, and the mere mention of Pendle is enough to evoke visions of witchery and black magic. The aura of witches so pervades the area that you can scarce travel a mile without thinking of them.

But there's more – much more – to Pendle than witches. For many folk the image of Lancashire is one of brash seaside resorts and dismal terraced streets in grimy mill towns, but the walker in Pendle will discover a Lancashire rich in natural beauty; a region which offers an exciting range of attractions varied enough to suit all conceivable tastes and interests :-

- wild, windswept, gritstone moorlands, whose moods alter with every subtle change of light and shade
- green and fertile valleys, with shady woodlands and exquisitely beautiful riverside walks
- gently rolling farmland, with patchwork fields and flowery meadows
- sparkling streams rushing and tumbling down deep, wooded cloughs
- picturesque villages, historic buildings and hoary old farmsteads – each with a story to tell
- extensive and panoramic views
- relics of ancient civilizations
- shimmering lakes and reservoirs, nature reserves and country parks
- quiet, leafy lanes, canal towpaths, ancient packhorse trails and a vast network of public footpaths

In the course of my exploratory wanderings I have talked with many farmers and local folk – good-natured people all, whose warm friendliness and kind help I have greatly appreciated.

In this modern life of bustle and stress there is no better form of escapism than a country walk. Whether you walk for bodily exercise, relaxation of the mind, or the enjoyment of natural scenery and places of interest, you will not be disappointed by what Pendle has to offer.

But enough of this. If you were born and bred in this area, as I was, you will love it and not need me to extol its virtues. If, on the other hand, you've not yet discovered Pendleside, then it's really time you did something about it. So get your boots on and give it a try – you'll be bewitched !

J. Keighley

December 1991

THE PENDLE WAY

The possibility of creating a long-distance walk in the area was first mooted in 1985. A working party was set up, headed by Pendle Borough Council and including Pendle Enterprise Trust, Pendle Heritage Centre and the Manpower Services Commission. Construction work, grant-aided by the Countryside Commission, began in July 1986, and the resultant 'Pendle Way' is a 45-mile circular walk around the Borough of Pendle, with waymarkers featuring a witch and yellow arrow. Those interested in walking this splendid route could not do better than purchase a set of informative leaflets 'The Pendle Way' (grant-aided by the Countryside Commission and designed and written by Pendle Heritage Centre). These describe the route in clockwise direction, covering the walk in 8 sections. The starting-points of each section are shown on the map.

●●●●●● Sections of Pendle Way which coincide with walks in this book

6

The Pendle Witches

The dramatic and complex story of the Pendle Witches unfolded during the spring and summer of the year 1612. It is a story which has left an indelible mark on the countryside around Pendle, which will be forever known as the 'Hill of the Witches.' Pendleside visitors will very soon become aware of the light-hearted sort of 'witch cult' which has developed in the area ; there was nothing light-hearted, however, about the witch-hunt which led to the public hanging of ten wretched individuals — eight women and two men — at Lancaster on 20th. August 1612.

Who or what were these so-called Pendle Witches? Certainly they were *not* witches of the classic (black cloak, pointed hat, black cat, whizzing about on broomstick) tradition. In the main they were ignorant peasants – social outcasts – scraping a meagre living by begging and stealing. They probably believed — or half-believed — that they were witches, with special powers, and the drugs, such as belladonna and aconite, which they no doubt took may well have induced such delusions. They also knew that if they could convince the local populace of their power to kill or maim through witchcraft then they could use threats and blackmail to demand what they wanted from anyone they chose. In this respect they had the advantage of living in an age when there was a great deal of superstition, a general belief in witchcraft and an irrational fear of the supernatural.

In 1612 there were two notable families of 'witches' in the area — The Demdike Brood and the Chattox Clan — and their respective senior members were the two most feared local witches. Both would be about eighty at this time, and both were withered, decrepit, sightless old crones. Mother Demdike (real name Elizabeth Southernes) lived at Malkin Tower, where she brought up her children and grandchildren as practising witches. Her daughter, Elizabeth Device, was, besides being mentally depraved, an exceedingly ugly creature (she was nicknamed 'Squintin' Lizzie). Also in residence at Malkin Tower were Elizabeth's dim-witted son James, her wild and emotional daughter Alizon and a younger daughter, Jennet, who was only nine years old in 1612. Old Chattox lived in a hovel at Greenhead, near Fence. Her real name was Anne Whittle (the nickname 'Chattox' came from her maiden name of Chadwick). This repulsive old hag, who was given to ceaseless and incomprehensible prattle, had two daughters - Elizabeth (Bessie) Whittle and Anne Redfearne. There was bitter enmity between the two families, who terrorized each other as well as the rest of Pendle.

On the 18th. March 1612 Alizon Device set off for Trawden on a begging expedition. Near Colne she met one John Law, a Halifax pedlar, whom she asked for some pins. When the pedlar refused, Alizon began to curse him vehemently, and instructed a black dog, which had suddenly appeared on the scene, to attack him. Law collapsed, and was carried, 'paralysed and bereft of speech' into a nearby ale-house.

His son, Abraham, was summoned from Halifax to investigate the incident, and as a result of his inquiries Alizon, James and Elizabeth Device were commanded to appear, on the 30th. March, before Roger Nowell Esq., Magistrate, of Read Hall.

Nowell was an expert in complex legal matters, and was a skilled, if unscrupulous, interrogator. He also had a strong belief in, and fear of, witchcraft. Under pressure, Alizon not only confessed to being a witch, but also incriminated her grandmother, Demdike. The black dog at Colne, Alizon insisted, was her 'familiar' (No self-respecting witch would be without a 'familiar' – a demon or spirit, usually in animal form, attendant upon the witch and obeying her commands. The black cat is the classic 'familiar'). James gave evidence against his sister who, at the end of the proceedings, was detained in custody, whilst James and his mother were released.

Further dubious evidence found its way to Nowell, and on the 2nd. April Demdike, Chattox and Anne Redfearne were interrogated at Ashlar House, Fence. Demdike confessed to witchcraft and denounced Chattox (who also confessed) and Anne. On the 4th. April all three of them, together with Alizon, were taken via Bowland to Lancaster Castle, there to await trial under the Witchcraft Act of 1604.

Six days later, on Good Friday, a Witches' Assembly and Feast was held at Malkin Tower. Among those present were Elizabeth, James and Jennet Device, Christopher Howgate (Demdike's son) and his wife, Alice Nutter of Roughlee, Jane Bulcock and her son John, of Moss End Farm, Newchurch, Katherine Hewet (known as 'Old Mouldheels') of Colne, Alice Grey, also of Colne and Jennet Preston of Gisburn. Alice Nutter was quite unlike the others in that she was a gentlewoman – well-educated and wealthy. Jannet Preston had just been acquitted at York Assizes of a charge of witchcraft.

When news of this Good Friday gathering reached the ears of Roger Nowell it was embroidered with some highly fanciful allegations. The witches, it was said, were planning to 'spring' their four colleagues from Lancaster Gaol and, furthermore, were plotting to blow up the Castle and murder the gaoler, Thomas Covell. Most of those who attended the Witches' Feast were rounded up for questioning, during the course of which James and Jennet Device gave damning evidence – some of it against their own family. James and his mother Elizabeth confessed to being involved in witchcraft, and all but one of the accused were bundled off to Lancaster to be tried at the August Assizes. The exception was Jennet Preston, the Gisburn witch. As Gisburn was then in Yorkshire she was sent for trial at York, where she was found guilty and hanged on the 29th. July.

On the 16th. August Sir Edward Bromley and Sir James Altham travelled from York to Lancaster to sit in judgement of nineteen indicted witches. The leading lady, however, didn't make it, for Old Demdike had died in her cell. Roger Nowell was Prosecutor, and Thomas Potts came from London to act as Clerk of Court. His copious records were to form the basis of a book 'The Wonderfull Discoverie of Witches in the Countie of

8

Lancaster' which was published in 1613.

To say that the trial was one-sided would be an understatement. The defendants had no professional representation, and most of the evidence offered would today have been totally unacceptable. In addition to this, the 'star' witness for the prosecution was the nine-year-old Jennet Device. So self-assured and word perfect was she that there seems little doubt that she had been carefully primed, coached and brain-washed.

Ten of the 'Pendle Witches' were found guilty, and nine of them – Old Chattox, Elizabeth, James and Alizon Device, Anne Redfearne, John and Jane Bulcock, Alice Nutter and Katherine Hewet – went to the gallows at Lancaster on the 20th. August 1612, together with one Isabel Robey of Widnes. Margaret Pearson, of Padiham, who was prosecuted by Nicholas Bannister, was sentenced to stand in the pillory (on market days) at Clitheroe, Whalley, Padiham and Lancaster before serving a one year's term of imprisonment. Alice Grey was acquitted.

In 1633 there was a further outbreak of supposed witchcraft at Hoarstones, Fence. Seventeen (including Jennet Device) were sentenced to death, but reprieved by the King (Charles I).

Note: The names of the 'witches' in this account are as spelt by Potts in his records of the Lancashire Summer Assizes. In some cases the accuracy is open to doubt (e.g. 'Device' was very probably 'Davies').

9

PENDLE HILL

'Penighent, Pendle Hill, Ingleborough,
Three such hills be not all England through.
I long to climbe up Pendle ; Pendle stands
Rownd cop, survaiying all ye wilde moorelands.'

These words, written by the parson/poet Richard James during his 1636 tour of Lancashire, illustrate the impact which Pendle Hill had, and still has, on its beholders.

But why should this be so? Pendle is not a great mountain ; in fact it is not a mountain at all, its summit failing by 169 feet to attain that distinction. In general appearance it rather resembles an upturned boat — plain and simple and somewhat dull. It lacks the rugged sort of profile displayed by the aforementioned Penyghent and Ingleborough, and has none of the bristling crags and soaring arêtes of the volcanic hills of Cumbria. In truth, Pendle Hill is a very ordinary, common or garden fell, so why should it be so famous?

The answer lies in its geographical position, for Pendle stands in complete isolation between the main South Pennine Chain and the rolling Bowland Fells. Thus, having no competition, it rises majestically and appears much higher than it really is. It is instantly recognisable when viewed from any angle, and it dominates the surrounding countryside to a greater extent than does, perhaps, any other hill in the land.

What Pendle lacks in height it certainly makes up for in girth, for it is no less than seven miles in length and covers an area of about twenty-five square miles. The hill looks at its best when sun and clouds conspire to dapple its slopes with ever-changing patterns of light and shade, but it is a moody giant, and on a dull, cheerless day can appear sullen and sombre. Legends of witchcraft and black magic, strange superstitions and whispered tales of supernatural happenings have given Pendle an almost mystical atmosphere. Pass close to the hill on a wild, drab winter's day and you half-expect to catch sight of a black-cloaked, besom-mounted witch gliding silently by.

Pendle Hill has kept its size and shape because of its summit layer of hard, weather-resistant gritstone. The top of the hill is a vast, flat plateau of peat hags and coarse grasses. From the breezy summit the view must be one of the finest in England — a magnificent panorama of infinite variety and charm. Especially dramatic and beautiful is the prospect to the north-west across the Forest of

10

Bowland towards Lancaster (where the Pendle Witches languished and died) and the distant, hazy hills of Lakeland. Equally delightful is the Northern aspect, looking along Ribblesdale to the 'Three Peaks' and Yorkshire's limestone country. To the North-East are the Craven Fells, whilst close-at-hand to the East and South lies a string of Lancashire mill towns - Colne, Barrowford, Nelson, Brierfield, Burnley, Padiham and Accrington. Far away to the South-West, beyond the Mersey estuary, lie the mountains of Snowdonia, whilst finally, in the West, you may see the glint of the sun on the Irish Sea and even that much-sought landmark Blackpool Tower.

You will, of course, be very fortunate indeed to find yourself standing atop Pendle on a day clear enough for you to behold all these wonders.

Over the ages this brooding old hill has silently witnessed a whole pageant of human history. At the dawn of civilisation, when the valleys were heavily wooded and marshy, our early Bronze Age ancestors made their homes on Pendle's upper slopes. To this wild country came the Brigantes — a hardy and warlike Iron Age race — and the Romans, who established an important military centre at nearby Ribchester. The Normans constructed a castle on a limestone knoll at Clitheroe, and by the 13th century clearings (booths) were being cut in the forests and small cattle farms (vaccaries) were being set up. The great cavalcade of history flowed on through Pendle's shadows ; the Wars of the Roses, the Civil War and the witches came in turn, left their mark and were gone. In those far-off days Pendle was a link in a chain of beacons, and many a bonfire has blazed on its summit in times of trouble or celebration. One of the biggest was lit in June 1887, when over a thousand loyal subjects gathered on Pendle to celebrate Queen Victoria's Jubilee. Generations of mill workers, seeking respite from the grimy streets of nearby cotton towns, found recreation and rural pleasure on the slopes of Pendle, and thus pioneered the pastime of hill-walking which today has so very many adherents.

The affection with which local people have regarded dear old Pendle throughout history is nowhere better expressed than in the words of Nicholas Assheton in Harrison Ainsworth's classic novel 'The Lancashire Witches':-
' I love Pendle Hill, and from whatever side I view it — whether from this place (Whalley Nab), where I see it from end to end, from its lowest point to its highest, from Padiham, where it frowns upon me, from Clitheroe, where it smiles, or from Downham, where it rises in full majesty before me — from all points and under all aspects, whether robed in mist or radiant with sunshine. Born beneath its giant shadow, I look upon it with filial regard. Its broad, round, smooth mass is better than the roughest, craggiest, shaggiest, most sharply-splintered mountain of them all. And then what a view it commands! There is no hill in England like Pendle Hill!

11

PENDLE HERITAGE CENTRE

PARK HILL, BARROWFORD, NELSON BB9 6JQ   TEL (0282) 695366

The centre is based at historic Park Hill, the former home of the Bannister family of which the most famous member is Dr. Roger, the 4-minute miler. The Bannisters first settled here c 1450, but the oldest surviving parts of the house are 16th. C. A continuing programme of restoration has preserved these buildings and converted them to house exhibitions about the history of the site and of the Pendle area.

There is a video about the infamous Pendle witches, a 15th C style cruck barn and a re-created 18th C walled garden. The Shop has a wide range of books on local history, architecture, gardening and walking, plus an assortment of gifts and souvenirs. The Tea Room offers a selection of home-made cakes and scones. There is a free car park.

OPENING TIMES : 1st March - 20th December
Tue - Fri 10·00 - 4·30
Weekends and Bank Holidays 2·00 - 4·30

LOCAL INFORMATION CENTRES

NELSON : 20 Scotland Rd., Nelson BB9 7UU
Tel: (0282) 692890

BARNOLDSWICK : The Old Library, Fernlea Ave.,
Barnoldswick BB8 5DW   Tel : (0282) 817046

BURNLEY : Burnley Mechanics, Manchester
Rd., Burnley BB11 1JA   Tel : (0282) 30055

CLITHEROE : Council Offices, Church Walk,
Clitheroe BB7 2RA   Tel : (0200) 25566

COLNE : Bank House, Albert Rd., Colne BB8 0BP
Tel : (0282) 865500

BARLEY : Tel : (0282) 601893

ABOUT THIS BOOK

THE WALKS All the walks described in this book are circular, and begin at a place where a car may be parked without causing an obstruction. They are fairly uniform in length, an average of about 6 miles making them half-day rather than full-day excursions. Though not every place visited has a known direct link with 'witchcraft', all the walks have starting points within 8 miles (as the broomstick flies) of the summit of Pendle Hill, and thus lie exclusively in that small corner of Lancashire(*) where local 'witchlore' prevails. The routes are almost entirely public rights-of-way, with occasional recourse to commonly-used tracks in open country. They should be free from serious difficulty, and well within the capability of reasonably fit and agile walkers.

Walk 19 briefly trespasses into Yorkshire

THE MAPS The strip-maps show all relevant route-finding features. All the routes have been walked and surveyed in detail by the author, and great care has been taken to ensure accuracy, although for the sake of clarity there is deliberate distortion of scale in depicting routes along, for example, narrow lanes, or through farmyards. Changes, however, will occur quite frequently, particularly on low-level routes across farmland, where the walker may expect to encounter new stiles and fences and sometimes diversions, either temporary or permanent. In such cases please note and obey legitimate waymarks and signs. In the Route Directions, any mention of a gate, stile or footbridge means that it is used, unless otherwise stated. The maps and route directions should suffice to guide walkers safely around the chosen routes. Nevertheless it is strongly recommended that an Ordnance Survey map be carried, as this will add interest and enable the walker to identify distant features not mentioned in the text. Almost all the walks are covered by four O.S. PATHFINDER (1:25 000) MAPS, viz :-

    669 (SD 64/74) Clitheroe and Chipping
    670 (SD 84/94) Barnoldswick and Earby
    680 (SD 63/73) Longridge and Great Harwood
    681 (SD 83/93) Burnley

Also used : 660 (SD 65/75) Slaidburn and Forest of Bowland (Walk 7); 661 (SD 85/95) Skipton and Hellifield (Walk 30).

The O.S. LANDRANGER (1:50 000) MAP 103 Blackburn and Burnley covers the entire area and is invaluable to both walker and motorist.

WALKING IN WITCH COUNTRY
A FEW WORDS OF ADVICE

- Many of the routes in this book cross agricultural land, and farmers will not welcome inconsiderate visitors. When crossing fields keep closely to paths and walk in single file across meadowland. Avoid climbing walls, and securely close all gates behind you, unless they are obviously meant to be left open.

- Leave no litter.

- Dogs must be kept on a lead in the proximity of livestock. This is especially vital during lambing time (March to May).

- Cars must not be parked where they obstruct field gates or cause damage to grass verges. Lock your car securely and hide from view any attractive or valuable items (or take them with you).

- Some of the routes described in this book cross high, exposed moorland terrain where the weather conditions can change very quickly. It should not be assumed that, because it's a nice warm day at valley level, it will necessarily be so at, say, the summit of Pendle. If the weather turns nasty, don't hesitate to call it a day and return by the route along which you came.

- When walking along a motor road walk on the right to face the oncoming traffic. The exception to this is on approaching a blind bend, where it may be necessary to cross to the left for a clear view.

- Before setting out, try to let others know where you're going (especially if you're walking alone).

CLOTHING AND EQUIPMENT Boots or strong, comfortable shoes are essential (on the high moors and in winter boots are the only suitable footwear). A windproof jacket or anorak (preferably with a hood) will be needed. Thick, heavy sweaters are not recommended – two or three lightweight layers are warmer and more adaptable to changing conditions. Denim is not at all suitable. In cold weather a woollen hat or cap will prevent the loss of a great deal of body heat.

A walking-stick is a matter of personal preference. Some walkers wouldn't be seen dead with one, but the author's constant companion is a hazel knobstick, which he finds useful for very steep, slippery descents, fording streams, beating down nettles, discouraging aggressive animals and testing potentially boggy ground prior to sinking in up to the knees. (A stick can be a nuisance on a route which involves

14

steep rock-scrambling, but there are none of those in this book). A rucsac is needed. A small 'daysac' with a capacity of about 20 litres would be adequate for any of these walks. The author's rucsac will always contain the following items :-

- waterproof cagoule and overtrousers
- spare woollen pullover
- small first-aid kit
- large-scale O.S. map
- compass
- whistle
- plastic bottle for water or cold drink
- a high-calorie snack (usually chocolate or crisps)
- windproof lighter for getting the old briar going (the alternative being about 10 boxes of matches

To these basic items may be added a pair of gloves and a flask containing hot coffee or soup.

CHILDREN When taking children on country walks some thought must be given to the distance and the type of terrain involved. Until you are sure of the child's capabilities, keep the distances short. Most of the walks in this book would probably be too much for a child under the age of five. As a rough rule of thumb, a child should be able to manage about a mile for each year of his age after his fifth birthday. Children should be warmly clothed and well shod. One cannot always afford to buy expensive boots for growing feet, but at least the child should have strong shoes or close-fitting wellingtons. On no account should young children be allowed to wander off beyond the range of vision of responsible adults, and extreme care and control must be exercised in the vicinity of crags, quarries and canals.

15

THE WALKS

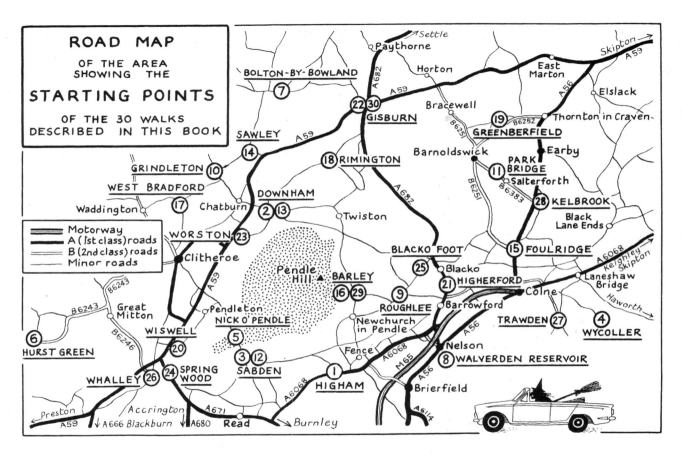

ROAD MAP
OF THE AREA
SHOWING THE
STARTING POINTS
OF THE 30 WALKS
DESCRIBED IN THIS BOOK

Motorway
A (1st class) roads
B (2nd class) roads
Minor roads

Settle
Paythorne
Skipton
BOLTON-BY-BOWLAND
Horton
East Marton
Elslack
Bracewell
GISBURN
Thornton in Craven
GREENBERFIELD
SAWLEY
Barnoldswick
Earby
GRINDLETON
RIMINGTON
PARK BRIDGE
Salterforth
WEST BRADFORD
DOWNHAM
KELBROOK
Waddington
Chatburn
Black Lane Ends
WORSTON
Twiston
Clitheroe
BLACKO FOOT
FOULRIDGE
Pendle Hill
Blacko
Keighley Skipton
Great Mitton
BARLEY
HIGHERFORD
Laneshaw Bridge
Colne
Pendleton
ROUGHLEE
Barrowford
Haworth
NICK O'PENDLE
Newchurch in Pendle
TRAWDEN
WYCOLLER
WISWELL
Nelson
HURST GREEN
SPRING WOOD
SABDEN
Fence
WALVERDEN RESERVOIR
WHALLEY
HIGHAM
Brierfield
Preston
Accrington
Read
Burnley
A666 Blackburn
A680

17

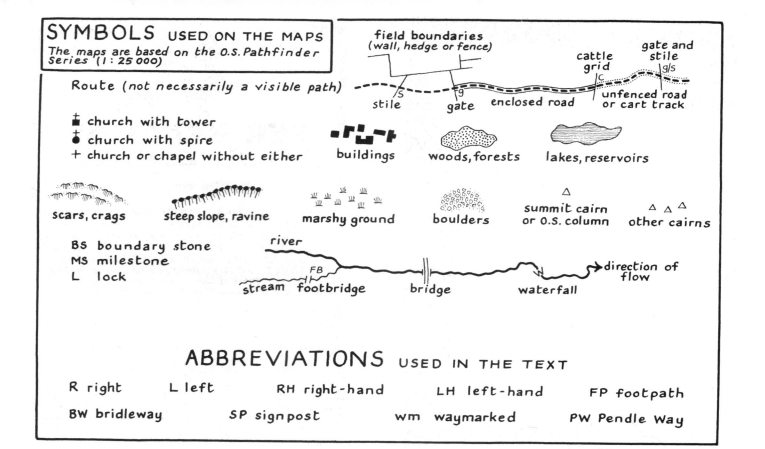

SYMBOLS USED ON THE MAPS

The maps are based on the O.S. Pathfinder Series (1:25 000)

field boundaries (wall, hedge or fence)

cattle grid

gate and stile

Route (not necessarily a visible path)

stile

gate

enclosed road

unfenced road or cart track

☐ church with tower
● church with spire
+ church or chapel without either

buildings

woods, forests

lakes, reservoirs

scars, crags

steep slope, ravine

marshy ground

boulders

summit cairn or O.S. column

other cairns

BS boundary stone
MS milestone
L   lock

river

stream

FB
footbridge

bridge

waterfall

direction of flow

ABBREVIATIONS USED IN THE TEXT

R right   L left   RH right-hand   LH left-hand   FP footpath

BW bridleway   SP signpost   wm waymarked   PW Pendle Way

18

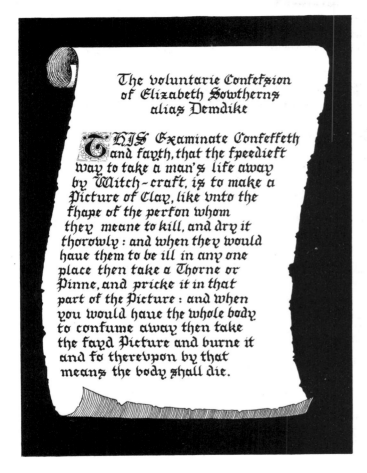

The voluntarie Confeſſion
of Elizabeth Sowtherns
alias Demdike

THIS Examinate Confeſſeth and ſayth, that the ſpeedieſt way to take a man's life away by Witch-craft, iſ to make a Picture of Clay, like vnto the ſhape of the perſon whom they meane to kill, and dry it thorowly : and when they would haue them to be ill in any one place then take a Thorne or Pinne, and pricke it in that part of the Picture : and when you would haue the whole body to confume away then take the ſayd Picture and burne it and ſo therevpon by that meanſ the body ſhall die.

THE HEART OF WITCH COUNTRY

7¼ MILES

Scenically the least attractive walk in the book, but given pride-of-place because of its many connections with the Pendle Witches. From Higham, where dwelt the ghastly Chattox and several of her 'victims', the route takes in Greenhead (scene of the witches' earliest foul deeds), Hoarstones (alleged haunt of witches in 1633) and Ashlar House (where witches were interrogated prior to being despatched to Lancaster and the gallows).

Ashlar House, Fence

PARKING At extreme E end of Higham village, adjacent to main A6068, is short section of obsolete road. Cars and broomsticks can be parked here. *Map ref: 813 367*

ROUTE DIRECTIONS ① Walk into village. Just past church turn L through stile (PW sign) and go down to main road. ② Turn L, and in 60 yds take stile on R (PW sign). Bear slightly L across field to stile into tarmac lane. Turn R. ③ After passing through gate/stile ignore farm road going to R. Keep straight on, following obvious track downhill to river. ④ Just before reaching footbridge turn L over stile. Clear path soon fades. Keep roughly parallel to river. ⑤ Cross stile and footbridge near big bend of river and follow clear path through wooded area to stile. Keep straight on along broad path. Cross drive, stile and footbridge, then straight on up far bank to follow LH field boundary. ⑥ Cross to L of fence for access to motorway bridge. Immediately across bridge turn L across field to stile/steps onto road. Turn L. ⑦ Turn R into drive of Newlaund Farm. Pass to L of farm and straight on along rough lane. ⑧ Turn R at far side of cottages, then bear L down to footbridge. Cross stile beyond and bear slightly R to climb to farm. Through stile to cross small lawn (carefully), then turn L. Follow farm drive to lane and turn R. ⑨ Just before reaching motorway turn L along lane. At bottom of hill turn L along another lane (FP sign). ⑩ After passing weir keep L at fork to follow tarmac lane up through woods and straight on to Old Laund Hall. Continue forward along cart-track. ⑪ On reaching gate go through gap-stile on L and follow RH hedge. Cross road to stile and path. ⑫ At top of field turn R and first L, then L again along road through Wheatley Lane. ⑬ Take stile on R opposite 'Laund View' (bungalow). Pass to R of large house ahead, and climb as far as third telegraph pole. Turn L along hillside and R up drive. ⑭ Turn L along lane. ⑮ Opposite Newchurch road turn L through gate and down path to continue along housing estate

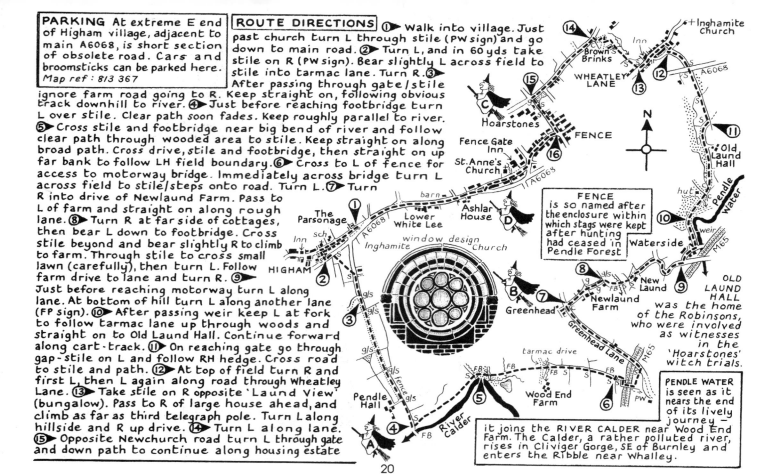

FENCE is so named after the enclosure within which stags were kept after hunting had ceased in Pendle Forest

OLD LAUND HALL was the home of the Robinsons, who were involved as witnesses in the 'Hoarstones' witch trials.

PENDLE WATER is seen as it nears the end of its lively journey — it joins the RIVER CALDER near Wood End Farm. The Calder, a rather polluted river, rises in Cliviger Gorge, SE of Burnley and enters the Ribble near Whalley.

20

road. Where road turns L, keep straight on down 'snicket' at corner. ⑯► Turn R along Wheatley Lane Road. Bear L at junction (Padiham 3½), then turn R along continuation of Wheatley Lane Road. Turn R along main A6068.

HIGHAM is partly industrialised but has some very attractive old cottages. The Four Alls Inn displays an unusual sign and has an interesting horse-trough.

PENDLE HALL
is Victorian, but is built 17thC style and incorporates several features of the much older house which it replaced. Chattox, one of the most infamous witches, and her daughter, Anne Redfearne, are thought to have lived near here, in a squalid hovel close to the river.

GREENHEAD
At the Lancaster Witch Trials of 1612, Chattox and Anne Redfearne were found guilty of causing by witchcraft the deaths of, respectively, Robert Nutter and his father Christopher. Robert and Christopher, of Greenhead had, on their deathbeds some 18 years previously, claimed to have been bewitched.

The INGHAMITE CHURCH was the first (1750) to be built by followers of Rev. Benjamin Ingham. There are only 3 others in the world still open - two locally (Winewall and Salterforth) and one in Canada.

HOARSTONES
was where a boy claimed he was held prisoner by witches on Hallowe'en 1633. He named 17 of his captors, and trials were held in 1634. Some were gaoled, and 4 were sent to London to be shown to huge crowds.

ASHLAR HOUSE
On 2nd. April 1612 Demdike, Chattox and Anne Redfearne were interrogated here and sent for trial. On 27th. April Elizabeth, James and Jennet Device were also brought here for questioning.

O.S. PATHFINDER (1 : 25 000) MAP
Nº 681 (SD 83/93) Burnley

© Jack Keighley 1992

21

②

DOWNHAM & TWISTON

5 MILES

If you only ever do one walk from this book, make sure it's this one - preferably in late Spring or early Summer. You may scour the length and breadth of England, but you won't find a prettier walk. *Grander*, maybe, or more *spectacular*, but not *prettier*. Walk it slowly and savour it, for this is truly Arcadia.

Assheton Arms
Downham

J. Keighley

ROUTE DIRECTIONS

1 From car park entrance turn L to bridge, but don't cross it. Turn R along road, and in a few yards L along lane by stream. **2** At end of lane go through stile and continue by stream for about 150 yds before bearing R across field to stile just to R of small tributary stream. Follow this stream to a footbridge, cross it, and 100 yds further on go over stile in hedge on L. Cross field to farm, and enter farmyard by gate/stile just to L of main buildings. **3** Turn L to gate/stile in front of big barn. Bear R across field to long, wooded hollow, and climb alongside it to wall stile at top of field. **4** Curve L across big field to stile in wall. Cross farm road and straight on by fence to another stile. Straight on, passing R of barn, then turn R and follow tiny stream to farm. **5** Enter farmyard and keep L of all buildings to field gate. Beyond it turn R up farm track. Curve L to reach gate/stile in wall on R, then continue forward by fence on L to next farm. **6** Go through gate to R of farm and turn R up farm road. When wall on L ends, turn L and descend to stream and footbridge. **7** Bear slightly L up far bank to gap in wall. Keep straight on uphill, then curve R with stream to footbridge near barn. Go up by wall on L. **8** Turn L at near side of derelict cottage. Straight on past telegraph pole to slit stile, then follow hedge/fence on L down to gate/stile in corner. **9** Follow hedge on R round to gate, keep to LH side of narrow field to stile, then straight across field to gate/stile to L of buildings. **10** Head L across limestone pasture, gradually getting closer to wooded stream valley on L. Cross stile and descend to stream and footbridge. Over it, bear L to gate. **11** Turn R along lane. At first bend cross step stile on L and follow stream down to footbridge over Ings Beck. **12** Turn L and keep alongside stream until fence deflects you R to stile. Over it, head uphill towards fence on R and continue alongside it. **13** When fence makes a R turn leave it and descend L to follow stream down to footbridge. Cross it and continue forward between limestone knolls. **14** Pass through yard to L of house and along drive. Almost at end of drive go L over stile and up clear path heading to R of large

Map labels: Downham Bridge, Downham Mill, Rimington Lane, to Chatburn, large, wooded, limestone knoll, Downham Green, line of Roman road, DOWNHAM, toilets, car park, to Barley, Downham Beck, Clay House Farm, fence, wooded depression, Hollins Farm, barn, Hecklin Farm, road, farm track, Ravens Holme, Ings Beck, Torrid Bank Wood, Twiston Beck, don't cross this footbridge, Twiston Mill, mill pond, barn, TWISTON, Twiston Beck, Brownlow, barn

derelict cottage at point 8

22

wooded knoll. Path veers R and heads towards distant wood. ⑮► Pass L of wood to stile and follow wall on R down to village.

DOWNHAM

One of Lancashire's loveliest villages. DOWNHAM HALL has been occupied by the ASSHETONS since 1558. The Elizabethan mansion was extensively rebuilt in 1835 in classic Georgian style. Surprisingly, the beautiful ST. LEONARD'S CHURCH was built as recently as 1909-10 (except for the tower, which is 15th.C.) to replace a very plain building erected after the 15th.C. church was pulled down in 1800. There has been a church here, however, since at least 1283, and probably long before that - possibly even in Saxon times. The late Queen Mary regarded the view from the porch as the most beautiful from any church porch in the land. OLD WELL HALL, near the bridge, is a superb Tudor house, whilst grouped around the green are typical 18th. and 19th. C. HANDLOOM WEAVERS' COTTAGES. Downham and the Assheton family feature prominently in Harrison Ainsworth's famous novel 'THE LANCASHIRE WITCHES'. In 1961 the village was used as the location for 'WHISTLE DOWN THE WIND', an excellent film starring Hayley Mills.

Twiston Mill

TWISTON

is a small, scattered community of grey stone cottages and ancient farmsteads. The name is derived from 'Twyssultune', and opinion is divided as to whether this means 'a place where streams meet' or 'a town on a boundary'. The latter seems likely, for Ings Beck, until 1974, divided Lancashire and Yorkshire and, ages ago, formed part of the boundary between the Saxon kingdoms of Mercia and Northumbria. TWISTON COTTON MILL, waterwheel-driven, closed due to fire at the end of the last century.

O.S. PATHFINDER (1 : 25 000) MAPS
Nº 669 (SD 64/74) Clitheroe and Chipping
Nº 670 (SD 84/94) Barnoldswick and Earby

WALKS IN LANCASHIRE WITCH COUNTRY

③

OVER SPENCE MOOR

6½ MILES

Looming sombrely over the Sabden Valley is the sprawling hump of Spence Moor, and a walk over this southern flank of Pendle Hill will appeal to those with a taste for bleak and desolate places. But there is sylvan beauty too; notably in the wooded confines of Cock Clough and the park-like countryside around The Whins.

Churn Clough Reservoir

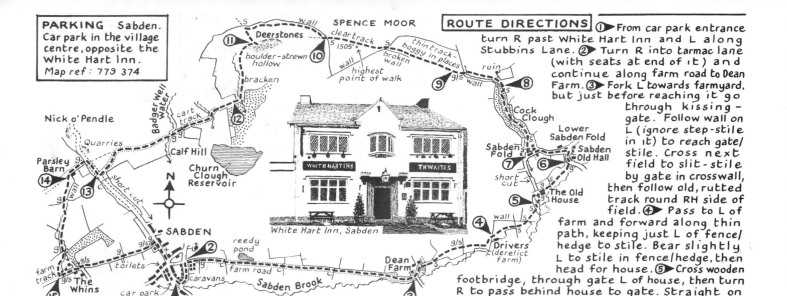

PARKING Sabden. Car park in the village centre, opposite the White Hart Inn. Map ref: 779 374

SPENCE MOOR

Deerstones

Nick o' Pendle

Badger Well Water

Quarries

Parsley Barn

Calf Hill

Churn Clough Reservoir

SABDEN

N

The Whins

car park

caravans

reedy pond

toilets

farm road

Sabden Brook

Dean Farm

Drivers (derelict farm)

Sabden Fold

Lower Sabden Fold

Sabden Old Hall

The Old House

Cock Clough

ruin

short cut

White Hart Inn, Sabden

WHITE HART INN   THWAITES

ROUTE DIRECTIONS ① From car park entrance turn R past White Hart Inn and L along Stubbins Lane. ② Turn R into tarmac lane (with seats at end of it) and continue along farm road to Dean Farm. ③ Fork L towards farmyard, but just before reaching it go through kissing-gate. Follow wall on L (ignore step-stile in it) to reach gate/stile. Cross next field to slit-stile by gate in crosswall, then follow old, rutted track round RH side of field. ④ Pass to L of farm and forward along thin path, keeping just L of fence/hedge to stile. Bear slightly L to stile in fence/hedge, then head for house. ⑤ Cross wooden footbridge, through gate L of house, then turn R to pass behind house to gate. Straight on to cross fence stile. Follow valley forward, then go up L to gate/stile in front of Sabden Old Hall. ⑥ Turn L up road and L at first road junction. ⑦ Pass farm, and when wall on R turns R go with it to fence stile. Keep R of stream to fence stile, then follow stream up through trees. After another fence stile, path climbs steep spur between two streams. Approaching top of wood look for stile on R. ⑧ Continue to climb alongside wood. Go through gateway and turn L to climb alongside gully on L to gate/stile. ⑨ Straight on (ENE) up rough moor to ladder-stile in crosswall. Over it a clearer path maintains direction to another ladder-stile. ⑩ Turn R (footpath sign) to follow wall on R. On reaching a ladder-stile in this wall don't cross it – turn sharp L along clear path. ⑪ At bouldery depression turn R, skirt rim of hollow and descend towards RH end of reservoir keeping to LH side of clough. Cross stream just above plantation. ⑫ Continue along clear path which soon develops into cart-track, crosses small stream and swings L then R to head for Nick o' Pendle. ⑬ Turn R up road, then L through metal gate onto farm road. ⑭ At far end of barn turn L off road and follow wall down to gate. Follow tiny stream down, keeping L of wall to gate, then descend to RH end of buildings. ⑮ Turn L along farm road and R along tarmac lane. When lane bends R, turn

24

L over step-stile by gate, then turn R to follow fence/hedge. Keep straight on to reach road and turn R.

IN MIST a compass may be needed, for Spence Moor is wide and featureless. The walk is not recommended in bad weather conditions.

SABDEN, a village with no pretensions to beauty, was industrialised by cotton manufacturer Richard Cobden in the 1820s. Cobden, a philanthropist who encouraged his employees to read, established a school and library in the village. The oldest part of Sabden is Heyhouses, to the north-east, which dates from the 16th. C. There are three churches – the Parish Church (built in 1846), the Baptist Church (1910) and the R.C. Church. The latter was built in the 1930s with stone from a demolished mill at Rochdale, at a total cost of £800. Today Sabden's main industries are printing, packaging and furniture-making.

Dean Farm was built in 1574, which makes it one of the oldest houses in the area. Above the lower set of mullioned windows is a lengthy and much-eroded inscription. The house has associations with the Lancashire Witch Trials of 1612.

Arrangement of mullioned windows, Dean Farm.

The derelict farmhouse of DRIVERS. Above the door is a datestone 1792.

O.S. PATHFINDER (1 : 25 000) MAPS
Nº 681 (SD 83/93) Burnley
Nº 680 (SD 63/73) Longridge and Great Harwood

© Jack Keighley 1992

THE VALE OF WYCOLLER

5¾ MILES

Wycoller, an ancient village rescued from seemingly inevitable dereliction, is one of Lancashire's prettiest and most romantic places. Here, where witch territory merges with Brontë country, you don't just *see* history – you *feel* it. Sparkling streams, flowery meadows, wild gritstone moors and wonderful views make this perhaps the best of several delightful walks available from Wycoller.

packhorse bridge, Wycoller

J Keighley

PARKING Wycoller Country Park has two car parks – Haworth Road and Trawden Lane. Use the latter, reaching it by leaving the A6068 at either Colne or Laneshaw Bridge.
Map ref: 927 395
Note: Motor cars, save for those of residents, essential services and disabled badge holders, are not allowed to progress beyond the car park.

great fireplace, Wycoller Hall

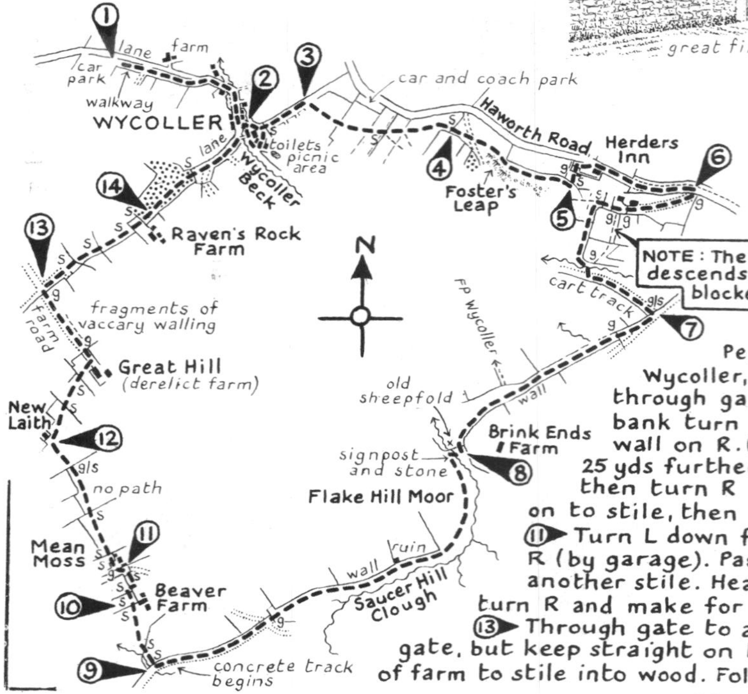

ROUTE DIRECTIONS ❶ Walk into village. ❷ Leave village either by steps to L of Hall or green track between info. centre and toilets. Cross stile and climb by wall on L. ❸ Just before reaching sunken section of track turn R (wm). Go through gap in wall and bear very slightly L uphill. From next stile keep climbing L to pass round wall corner to ladder-stile. ❹ Straight on across farm road and up to top of rocks. Continue forward to pass to R of wall corner. Follow wall on L. ❺ At foot of short, steep descent take step stile on L and climb LH side of field to gates giving access to Herders Inn car park. Turn R along road. ❻ Turn R through gate (Higher Keystyles Farm) and down farm road. Pass in front of farm (see note), through gate and on to gated stile in wall. Turn L to follow wall down, ford stream and go up to cart track. Turn L along it. ❼ Turn R on broad track (Bridleway Trawden, Pendle Way), but in 80yds leave it to follow wall on R (FP Wycoller, Pendle Way) to gate. Follow wall on L. ❽ After passing through gateway ford stream to clear path up bank. At top of bank turn L and follow clear track which soon comes alongside wall on R. ❾ At bottom of depression track gains concrete surface. 25 yds further on turn R over wall stile. Forward over another stile then turn R up to farm. ❿ Use ladder-stile L of farm, straight on to stile, then R over ladder-stile and L alongside wall to next farm. ⓫ Turn L down farm road and almost immediately take small gate on R (by garage). Pass in front of house to stile then straight ahead to another stile. Head towards next farm. ⓬ Just before reaching farm turn R and make for next farm. On reaching it turn L along farm road. ⓭ Through gate to a crossroads of tracks and turn R. Track turns R to gate, but keep straight on by fence to stile and head for next farm. ⓮ Keep L of farm to stile into wood. Follow clear path through wood to lane back to Wycoller.

NOTE: The official right-of-way descends here but may be blocked (it was in May 1991)

Map labels: lane, farm, car park, walkway, WYCOLLER, Wycoller Beck, toilets, picnic area, lane, Raven's Rock Farm, fragments of vaccary walling, farm road, Great Hill (derelict farm), New Laith, no path, Mean Moss, Beaver Farm, concrete track begins, car and coach park, Haworth Road, Herders Inn, Foster's Leap, cart track, FP Wycoller, wall, old sheepfold, signpost and stone, Brink Ends Farm, Flake Hill Moor, ruin, Saucer Hill Clough, N

26

WYCOLLER

Eleven centuries ago Saxon farmers founded a settlement at Wycoller (the name means 'cattle farm among the alders'). During the 17th. and 18th. centuries the village became a busy and thriving handloom weaving centre, but fell into decline when the invention of power looms took the textile industry into town mills. In 1950 a society called 'Friends of Wycoller' was formed and began some restoration work on the deserted and decaying village. The task, however, was enormous, and the future for Wycoller seemed grim. Then, in 1973, Lancashire County Council acquired the estate and most of the village, which is now being gradually restored to its 19th. C. form. The ruined 16th. C. Hall (extended 1744, abandoned 1818) is considered to be the Ferndean Manor of Charlotte Brontë's 'Jane Eyre'. The packhorse bridge and the clam, or slab bridge both date back to at least the 16th. C. and several of the farms and cottages are of 16th. and 17th. C. vintage. The large barn next to the Hall is an Information Centre and local history museum.

This remote old house, high on the Haworth road, has been an inn for about 130 years.

HERDERS INN & FREE HOUSE

FOSTER'S LEAP – Two huge boulders, separated by a 7' gap. Supposedly named after one Foster Cunliffe, a relative of the Cunliffes of Wycoller Hall, who jumped safely (so it is said) from one boulder to the other. He must have been either mad or drunk. *DEFINITELY NOT RECOMMENDED*

VACCARY WALLING

Upright stone slabs erected to enclose a 'vaccary' (monastic cattle farm). Those seen on this walk were probably built in the 13th. C.

O.S. PATHFINDER (1:25,000) MAP

Nº 681 (SD 83/93) Burnley

© Jack Keighley 1992

5

THE ASCENT OF PENDLE HILL
FROM NICK O' PENDLE

6¼ MILES

With a starting point at 1000 feet, and no steep climbing involved, this is by far the easiest route to the top of Pendle. It's a grand walk, but not, however, one to be considered in bad weather conditions, for the entire journey lies across wild, windswept moorland totally exposed to the elements.

Wellsprings Inn, Nick o' Pendle

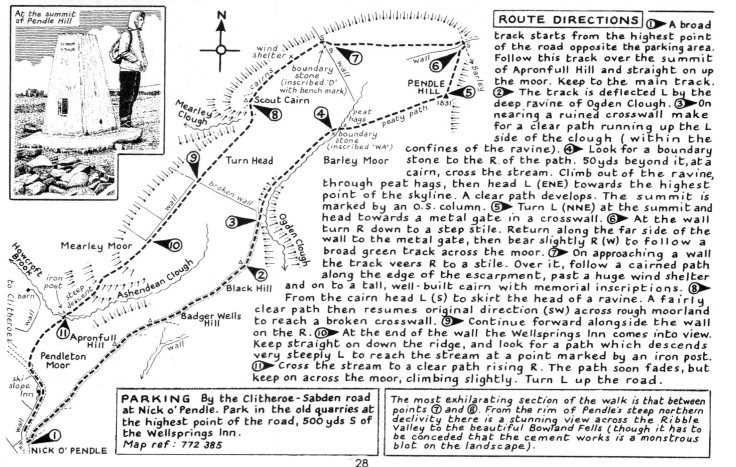

At the summit of Pendle Hill

ROUTE DIRECTIONS

① A broad track starts from the highest point of the road opposite the parking area. Follow this track over the summit of Apronfull Hill and straight on up the moor. Keep to the main track. ② The track is deflected L by the deep ravine of Ogden Clough. ③ On nearing a ruined crosswall make for a clear path running up the L side of the clough (within the confines of the ravine). ④ Look for a boundary stone to the R of the path. 50yds beyond it, at a cairn, cross the stream. Climb out of the ravine, through peat hags, then head L (ENE) towards the highest point of the skyline. A clear path develops. The summit is marked by an O.S. column. ⑤ Turn L (NNE) at the summit and head towards a metal gate in a crosswall. ⑥ At the wall turn R down to a step stile. Return along the far side of the wall to the metal gate, then bear slightly R (W) to follow a broad green track across the moor. ⑦ On approaching a wall the track veers R to a stile. Over it, follow a cairned path along the edge of the escarpment, past a huge wind shelter and on to a tall, well-built cairn with memorial inscriptions. ⑧ From the cairn head L (S) to skirt the head of a ravine. A fairly clear path then resumes original direction (SW) across rough moorland to reach a broken crosswall. ⑨ Continue forward alongside the wall on the R. ⑩ At the end of the wall the Wellsprings Inn comes into view. Keep straight on down the ridge, and look for a path which descends very steeply L to reach the stream at a point marked by an iron post. ⑪ Cross the stream to a clear path rising R. The path soon fades, but keep on across the moor, climbing slightly. Turn L up the road.

PARKING By the Clitheroe-Sabden road at Nick o' Pendle. Park in the old quarries at the highest point of the road, 500 yds S of the Wellsprings Inn.
Map ref: 772 385

The most exhilarating section of the walk is that between points ⑦ and ⑧. From the rim of Pendle's steep northern declivity there is a stunning view across the Ribble Valley to the beautiful Bowland Fells (though it has to be conceded that the cement works is a monstrous blot on the landscape).

TWO BOUNDARY STONES SEEN ON THE WALK

Point ④   Point ⑦

⊼ *BENCH MARK* An Ordnance Survey sign. It marks a spot where the height above sea-level has been accurately measured. The horizontal line above the arrowhead marks the exact altitude. When a surveyor takes other altitude measurements from the bench mark he fixes an angle-iron at the level of the horizontal line as a temporary bracket to support his instruments.

● ─ ● ─ ●

APRONFULL HILL is the highest point of Pendleton Moor, and an old local legend attempts to explain how it came by its unusual name. Apparently it was here that a rather nasty giant took a huge boulder from his apron and hurled it at Clitheroe Castle, knocking a gaping hole in the castle wall. The strain of perpetrating this mindless act of vandalism caused his apron strings to snap, spilling out the remaining boulders to form a ring of stones on the ground which remains there to this day.

cairn on Apronfull Hill

TAKE A COMPASS WITH YOU. MIST CAN DESCEND SUDDENLY ON PENDLE

O.S. PATHFINDER (1:25 000) MAPS
Nº 669 (SD 64/74) Clitheroe and Chipping
Nº 670 (SD 84/94) Barnoldswick and Earby
Nº 680 (SD 63/73) Longridge and Great Harwood

© Jack Keighley 1992

29

6

THREE RIVERS WALK

7¼ MILES

A lovelier riverside walk can scarce be imagined, for here, where the Hodder and Calder flow into and swell the Ribble, is some of the most beautiful countryside in Lancashire. A superb old packhorse bridge and a magnificent college in a glorious parkland setting are outstanding highlights of a walk which is a sheer joy from start to finish.

Cromwell's Bridge
River Hodder

JKeighley

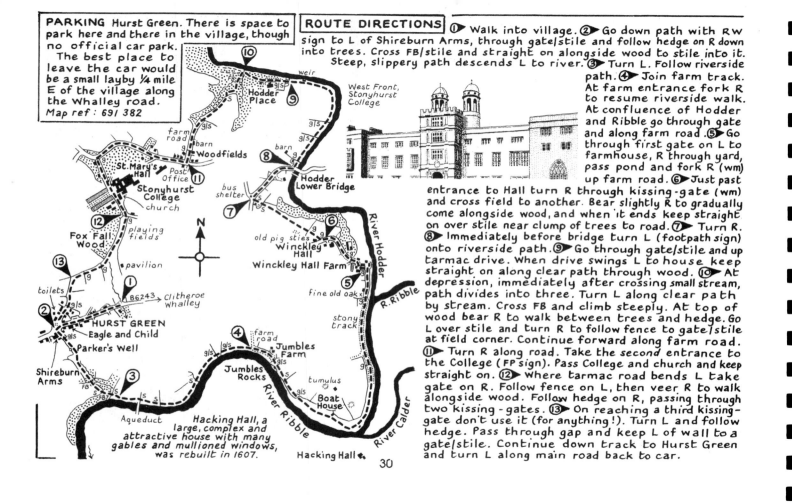

PARKING Hurst Green. There is space to park here and there in the village, though no official car park.
The best place to leave the car would be a small layby ¼ mile E of the village along the Whalley road.
Map ref: 691 382

ROUTE DIRECTIONS

① Walk into village. ② Go down path with RW sign to L of Shireburn Arms, through gate/stile and follow hedge on R down into trees. Cross FB/stile and straight on alongside wood to stile into it. Steep, slippery path descends L to river. ③ Turn L. Follow riverside path. ④ Join farm track. At farm entrance fork R to resume riverside walk. At confluence of Hodder and Ribble go through gate and along farm road. ⑤ Go through first gate on L to farmhouse, R through yard, pass pond and fork R (wm) up farm road. ⑥ Just past entrance to Hall turn R through kissing-gate (wm) and cross field to another. Bear slightly R to gradually come alongside wood, and when it ends keep straight on over stile near clump of trees to road. ⑦ Turn R. ⑧ Immediately before bridge turn L (footpath sign) onto riverside path. ⑨ Go through gate/stile and up tarmac drive. When drive swings L to house keep straight on along clear path through wood. ⑩ At depression, immediately after crossing small stream, path divides into three. Turn L along clear path by stream. Cross FB and climb steeply. At top of wood bear R to walk between trees and hedge. Go L over stile and turn R to follow fence to gate/stile at field corner. Continue forward along farm road. ⑪ Turn R along road. Take the second entrance to the College (FP sign). Pass College and church and keep straight on. ⑫ Where tarmac road bends L take gate on R. Follow fence on L, then veer R to walk alongside wood. Follow hedge on R, passing through two kissing-gates. ⑬ On reaching a third kissing-gate don't use it (for anything!). Turn L and follow hedge. Pass through gap and keep L of wall to a gate/stile. Continue down track to Hurst Green and turn L along main road back to car.

West Front, Stonyhurst College

Hodder Place
weir
farm road
barn
Woodfields
St. Mary's Hall
Post Office
Stonyhurst College
church
Fox Fall Wood
playing fields
pavilion
toilets
B6243 Clitheroe Whalley
HURST GREEN
Eagle and Child
Parker's Well
Shireburn Arms
Aqueduct

bus shelter
Hodder Lower Bridge
old pig sties
Winckley Hall
Winckley Hall Farm
fine old oak
stony track
River Hodder
River Ribble

farm road
Jumbles Farm
Jumbles Rocks
tumulus
Boat House
River Ribble
River Calder

Hacking Hall, a large, complex and attractive house with many gables and mullioned windows, was rebuilt in 1607.

Hacking Hall

30

THE HACKING FERRY

A ferry once operated across the Ribble near its confluence with the Calder, but was discontinued in 1954.

The boatman's house now stands empty and forlorn. An old ferry boat, found in a barn in 1983, was restored and can be seen in Clitheroe Castle Museum.

❀

The graceful arches of CROMWELL'S BRIDGE have spanned the Hodder since 1562. The bridge is so called because it is said that Cromwell marched his army across it en route for the Battle of Preston in August 1648.

❀

STONYHURST COLLEGE

This former Elizabethan mansion was begun in 1592 by Sir Richard Shireburn, the local landowner. In 1794 it was handed over, in a state of disrepair, to the Society of Jesuits. Since then the building has been extended, and is now one of England's most eminent public schools. In the college library are some priceless treasures, including books printed by Caxton and the oldest existing English bound book – a 7th.C. copy of St.John's Gospel. Sir Arthur Conan Doyle and the actor, Charles Laughton, are ex-pupils.

The walk offers an opportunity to observe a wide variety of waterside birds. Look out especially for the cormorant, which, though primarily a bird of coast and estuary, sometimes travels a fair distance inland along river valleys.

Cormorant

O.S. PATHFINDER (1:25 000) MAP Nº 680 (SD 63/73) Longridge and Great Harwood

© Jack Keighley 1992

31

WALKS IN LANCASHIRE WITCH COUNTRY

7

BOWLAND BYWAYS

7 MILES

Walkers may catch a glimpse of the deer which still roam this unspoilt and beautifully wooded countryside where the Ribble Valley merges with the verdant foothills of the magnificent Forest of Bowland. The ramble, from the idyllic village of Bolton-by-Bowland, passes a succession of splendid 17th C. farmsteads, whilst the views are exceptionally lovely.

Forest of Bowland

J.Keighley

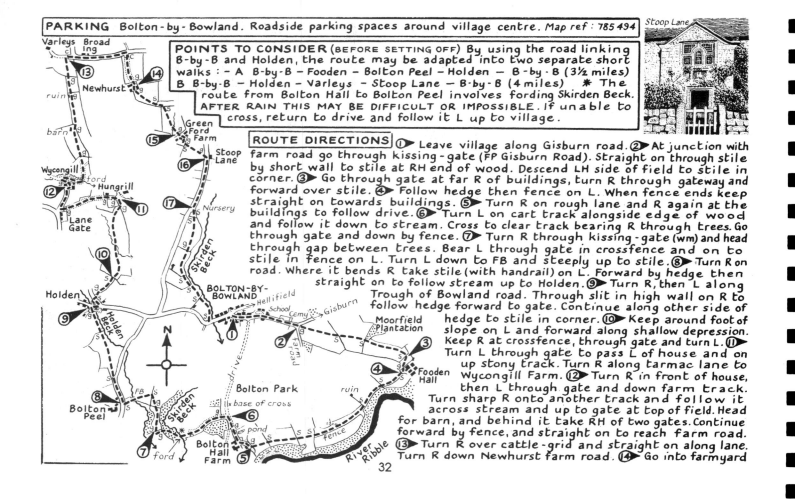

Stoop Lane

Varleys Broad Ing
c
13
14
Newhurst
ruin
barn
Green Ford Farm
15
Stoop Lane
16
Wycongill
ford
Hungrill
12
Lane Gate
11
17
Nursery
10
Skirden Beck
Holden
BOLTON-BY-BOWLAND
Holden Beck
Hellifield
9
School Cemy Gisburn
Moorfield Plantation
N
1
2
Farm road
3
4
Fooden Hall
drive
Bolton Park
ruin
8
FB
Skirden Beck
base of cross
Bolton Peel
6
pond
fence
7 ford
Bolton Hall Farm
5
River Ribble

POINTS TO CONSIDER (BEFORE SETTING OFF) By using the road linking B-by-B and Holden, the route may be adapted into two separate short walks :- A B-by-B – Fooden – Bolton Peel – Holden – B-by-B (3½ miles) B B-by-B – Holden – Varleys – Stoop Lane – B-by-B (4 miles) ✱ The route from Bolton Hall to Bolton Peel involves fording Skirden Beck. AFTER RAIN THIS MAY BE DIFFICULT OR IMPOSSIBLE. If unable to cross, return to drive and follow it L up to village.

ROUTE DIRECTIONS ①▸ Leave village along Gisburn road. ②▸ At junction with farm road go through kissing-gate (FP Gisburn Road). Straight on through stile by short wall to stile at RH end of wood. Descend LH side of field to stile in corner. ③▸ Go through gate at far R of buildings, turn R through gateway and forward over stile. ④▸ Follow hedge then fence on L. When fence ends keep straight on towards buildings. ⑤▸ Turn R on rough lane and R again at the buildings to follow drive. ⑥▸ Turn L on cart track alongside edge of wood and follow it down to stream. Cross to clear track bearing R through trees. Go through gate and down by fence. ⑦▸ Turn R through kissing-gate (wm) and head through gap between trees. Bear L through gate in crossfence and on to stile in fence on L. Turn L down to FB and steeply up to stile. ⑧▸ Turn R on road. Where it bends R take stile (with handrail) on L. Forward by hedge then straight on to follow stream up to Holden. ⑨▸ Turn R, then L along Trough of Bowland road. Through slit in high wall on R to follow hedge forward to gate. Continue along other side of hedge to stile in corner. ⑩▸ Keep around foot of slope on L and forward along shallow depression. Keep R at crossfence, through gate and turn L. ⑪▸ Turn L through gate to pass L of house and on up stony track. Turn R along tarmac lane to Wycongill Farm. ⑫▸ Turn R in front of house, then L through gate and down farm track. Turn sharp R onto another track and follow it across stream and up to gate at top of field. Head for barn, and behind it take RH of two gates. Continue forward by fence, and straight on to reach farm road. ⑬▸ Turn R over cattle-grid and straight on along lane. Turn R down Newhurst farm road. ⑭▸ Go into farmyard

32

and L to take LH of two gates. Follow RH side of field, over stile in corner, then cross tiny stream to stile on R. Head for farm. ⑮▶ Through metal gate into farmyard. Bear very slightly L between buildings and turn R behind barn to gate. Forward to wall stile on L and straight up field to gate in front of house. ⑯▶ Turn R along road. ⑰▶ Turn L over stile by sign 'Oaktree Nurseries' and follow fence. Over stile and straight along field about 60yds L of power line to small gate. Follow stream down to road and turn L into village.

BOLTON-BY-BOWLAND

Picturesque, non-commercialised, and with everything you might expect to find in the archetypal English village — hoary old church, village green (two in fact), cosy pub, market cross, stocks and quaint old cottages haphazardly set along the main street. The church is full of interest and must not be missed. Rebuilt c 1464 under the supervision of Sir Ralph Pudsay, whose tomb is quite remarkable. Fashioned in black Craven limestone, it depicts Sir Ralph and his three (consecutive !) wives, plus his twenty-five children. Each wife has, in the folds of her dress, a numeral indicating the number of children she bore to Sir Ralph — Matilda 2, Margaret 6 and Edwina 17. Many of the pews bear the date 1694 and the initials of their first owners. The studded oak door is dated 1705, and the large, octagonal font is early 16th.C.

—•—•—•—

BOLTON HALL, home of the Boltons (c 1129-1332) and Pudsays (1332-1770), was demolished in the 1960s, but some out-buildings remain. Henry VI stayed here in 1464 before moving on to Waddington (see Walk 17). From the Peel family of BOLTON PEEL came Sir Robert (Prime Minister 1834-5, 1841-6).

O.S. PATHFINDER (1:25 000) MAPS
Nº 669 (SD 64/74) Clitheroe and Chipping
Nº 660 (SD 65/75) Slaidburn and Forest of Bowland

© Jack Keighley 1992

WALVERDEN RESERVOIR

6¼ MILES

Rural charm and solitude at the very edge of East Lancashire's industrial sprawl. The walk begins but a stone's throw from Nelson's dreary terraced streets, and offers a wide variety of scenery ranging from the exposed uplands around Coldwell to the sheltered, leafy glades of Catlow Bottoms. Especially beautiful on a clear, frosty winter's day after a fall of snow.

PARKING Walverden Reservoir lies at the SE edge of Nelson. There is a sizeable car park below the reservoir dam, to which access is provided by a narrow, rough lane at the top of Brunswick Street. Map ref: 871 367

ROUTE DIRECTIONS

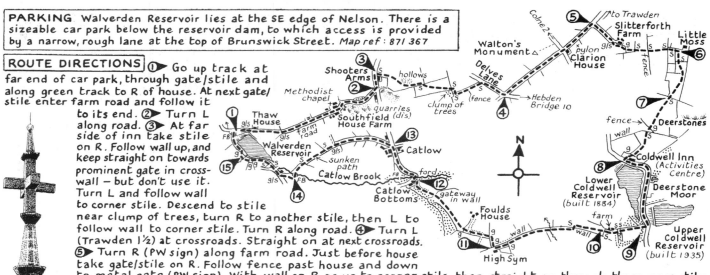

① Go up track at far end of car park, through gate/stile and along green track to R of house. At next gate/stile enter farm road and follow it to its end. ② Turn L along road. ③ At far side of inn take stile on R. Follow wall up, and keep straight on towards prominent gate in cross-wall — but don't use it. Turn L and follow wall to corner stile. Descend to stile near clump of trees, turn R to another stile, then L to follow wall to corner stile. Turn R along road. ④ Turn L (Trawden 1½) at crossroads. Straight on at next crossroads. ⑤ Turn R (PW sign) along farm road. Just before house take gate/stile on R. Follow fence past house and down to metal gate (PW sign). With wall on R go up to corner stile, then straight on through three more stiles. ⑥ Turn R (PW sign), over fence stile, then bear L to gateway in corner. Path continues by wall, then veers R to stile at far RH corner. ⑦ Climb hill ahead, keeping to R of highest point, to reach gate(wm) in fence. Cross corner to ladder-stile and descend to car park of Coldwell Inn. ⑧ Turn L along road. ⑨ At bottom of hill (just beyond reservoir) take wall stile (FP sign) on R. Up bank and follow trees on R to farm. Keep L of all buildings to ladder-stile. ⑩ Bear L uphill towards wall and follow it forward, crossing to other side of it at stile. Go through metal kissing gate and along overgrown track between walls. ⑪ At cottage turn R through gate. Follow wall on L to gate in it, then descend to join farm road. When this bends R keep straight on through gate and descend to R of wooded ravine to locate cart track down to road. ⑫ Turn R across ford and up lane to Catlow. ⑬ Turn L along rough lane (FP Nelson) and follow it to its end at a gate/stile. Straight on to corner stile, then descend sunken path to reach footbridge. ⑭ Cross bridge and turn R on clear path. At farm road turn R. When farm road bends L keep straight on over stiles and along gravel path. ⑮ Take gate on R to join lakeside path. Through gate and down steps to car park.

WALTON'S SPIRE, atop an ancient stone shaft, was placed here by the Reverend Richard Wroe-Walton, of Marsden Hall, in 1835. Blown down by gales in 1984, it was re-erected and an information panel was sited beside it.

34

NELSON is the largest and yet the youngest of all the settlements in Pendle. It grew from the villages of Great and Little Marsden, and took its name from the Nelson Inn in the town centre. The rapid growth of Nelson followed the coming of the railway in 1849, which brought the textile industry to the area.

WALVERDEN RESERVOIR, built in 1869, is designated as a Countryside Recreation and Wildlife Conservation Area. Many species of birds flourish here, particularly in the reedy shallows at the head of the lake. Botanists and lepidopterists will also find much of interest.

The tiny hamlet of SOUTHFIELD – a delightful place – has changed little since the 18th C. John Wesley preached here on 18th April 1786, following which William Sagar converted his barn into a Methodist chapel – dated 1797 and still in regular use.

Clarion House

John Wesley 1703-91
Founder of Methodism

CLARION HOUSE, lonely now and with a sad air of neglect, had its heyday in the early part of the century. When the Independent Labour Party launched its weekly newspaper 'The Clarion' in 1891, circulation was boosted by cycling clubs formed throughout the country. Clarion Houses, built by volunteers, provided refreshments for cyclists.

COLDWELL INN

The Coldwell Inn had been a roadside pub for 100 years when it closed in 1939. During the 1920s it was a notorious den for illegal drinking and gambling – 52 people were arrested at a raid in 1922. Now converted into an Activities Centre, the present building bears no resemblance to the original.

O.S. PATHFINDER (1:25000) MAP   No 681 (SD83/93 Burnley

© Jack Keighley 1992

9

NOGGARTH RIDGE & NEWCHURCH

4½ MILES

Of all the villages hereabouts, Newchurch-in-Pendle is the most closely associated with tales of witchcraft. Our route of approach lies along the low, grassy ridge of Noggarth, which provides easy walking and grand sweeping views. The return to Roughlee is by way of some of the loveliest scenery in Pendleside, ending with a riverside walk of exquisite charm.

Newchurch-in-Pendle
J Keighley

PARKING Roughlee. From the centre of the village drive along the Barley road. In a little less than ½ mile you will come to a roadside parking space on the river bank (at the end of some white railings). Park at right angles to the road.
Map ref: 839 399

FOR NOTES ON ROUGHLEE SEE WALK 21

ROUTE DIRECTIONS
① Walk up the road, cross the bridge, and follow the riverside path downstream. ② At a point about opposite the parked car the path veers R, through hawthorns, and climbs the hillside diagonally to reach a stile where the fence meets the wall. Maintain direction (clear path), and when above caravan site bear R up to stile in front of reservoir pump house. ③ Turn R and cross cattle-grid onto enclosed farm road. ④ When confronted by two gates, take the RH one and keep straight on alongside wall on L. ⑤ At Noggarth Cottage maintain direction along tarmac lane for 50 yds then turn right through gate/stile (FP sign). Bear L to go round end of wall (not through gate) and on to stile (wm). ⑥ Turn L on farm road but don't cross the cattle-grid. Turn R and follow fence. Keep straight on along ridge. There is no continuous path, but aim for the mast visible ahead, crossing a number of broken walls and then a line of stiles. ⑦ Pass to the R of the farm, and after next stile bear slightly R round wall corner and follow clear track to cottage and road. ⑧ Keep L along road. In 40 yds cross stile in railings on R and head L to stile. Turn R to follow farm road, with wall on R. ⑨ Immediately past first house turn R down farm road. ⑩ On reaching gate turn R through stile and follow wall to next farm. Just past farm turn L off drive to stile, then head up to stile in wall on skyline. Keep straight on towards church. ⑪ Turn L up road and R at junction (For detour to Faughs Quarry turn L along Well Head Road. Quarry is ¼ mile on R). ⑫ At Lamb Inn turn R down Jinny Lane. In 100 yds take stile on L and follow clear path up to stile into wood. Follow

Noggarth Cottage

main track straight through wood to stile at far end. Keep straight on to come alongside wall on L, and follow it down past wood to stile in corner. ⑬ Continue down with wall now on R. Cross green lane and descend, keeping L of quarry, to gate/stile. ⑭ Go down rough lane (SP Whitehough Outdoor Education Centre). Turn R through small gate at near end of bridge and follow riverside path downstream. ⑮ Pass to L of farmhouse and continue along path running between stream and wall. At bridge turn L along road towards Roughlee.

White Hough
to Barley
ROUGHLEE
green lane
quarry
Pendle Water
Heys Lane Plantation
Thorney Bank
caravans (millions of 'em)
Black Bank
reservoir
Lamb Inn
toilets
Ridgaling Farm
NEWCHURCH-IN-PENDLE
Higher Gray Stones
Noggarth Cottage
Well Head Road
school
quarry (disused)
broken walls
fence
Faughs
Moss End
flooded quarry (fenced and dangerous)
boggy field
broken wall
Ouzle Rock (farm)
Bull Hole
Sabden Brook
Spen Height (farm)
Tinedale Farm
mill
Mast
Higher Spen

NEWCHURCH - IN - PENDLE

The old houses of this quaint village, many of them tall and whitewashed, are seemingly perched precariously on a steep hillside. A chapel-of-ease was established here c 1529, but the present church was built in the 18th C., after which the village, hitherto called Goldshaw Booth, adopted the name of 'Newchurch'. In the tower's west wall is a strange symbol known as the 'Eye of God' - a carved stone containing some oval glass. Near the porch the family grave of the Nutters of Roughlee is called the 'Witch's Grave', for Alice Nutter is reputedly interred here. It is unlikely, however, that a 'witch' would be buried in consecrated ground. Another Pendle Witch - Chattox - was alleged to have desecrated graves in this churchyard to collect skulls and teeth. In the centre of the village is the famous gift shop 'Witches Galore' - a fascinating place.

'Witch's Grave'

THE MYSTERY OF MALKIN TOWER *

MALKIN TOWER was the home of the Demdike Brood and the 'general HQ' of the 'witches' in the area. It has long since disappeared; it was probably a broken-down hovel in 1612, and may have been destroyed after the Witch Trials of that year. No one knows exactly where the house was sited, but many historians believe that it stood between BULL HOLE and MOSS END.

This face is carved on a rock in FAUGHS QUARRY. It is thought to be a memorial to a quarryman killed here in an accident around the turn of the century.

These two farms both feature in the Pendle Witch story. At Bull Hole Demdike is said to have killed a sick cow after being paid by the farmer to cure it. Moss End was the home of John and Jane Bulcock, both hanged as witches in 1612.
*sounds like the title of an Enid Blyton 'Famous Five' story!

O.S. PATHFINDER (1 : 25 000) MAPS
Nº 670 (SD 84/94) Barnoldswick and Earby
Nº 681 (SD 83/93) Burnley

© Jack Keighley 1992

WALKS IN LANCASHIRE WITCH COUNTRY
10

GRINDLETON FELL

7¼ MILES

A rapturous ramble from the lush, wooded pastures of the Ribble Valley into the south-eastern fringes of the magnificent hill country known as the Forest of Bowland — the largest tract of unspoiled countryside in Lancashire. The views of Pendle and the Ribble Valley are exquisite, whilst the prospect northwards, across the plains to the Dales mountains, is quite stupendous.

The Buck Inn Grindleton

THE BUCK INN

Bolton-By- 3
Bowland
Gisburn 5¼
Settle 13¼

Chatbu
Clither
Waddin

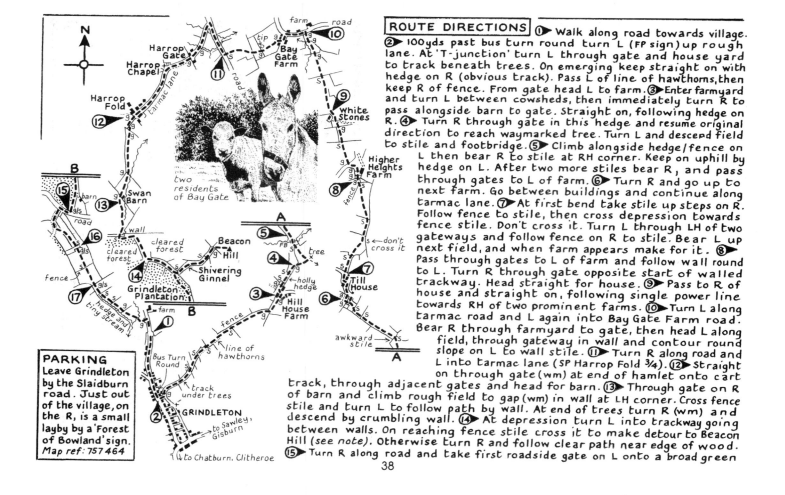

① ► Walk along road towards village. **② ►** 100yds past bus turn round turn L (FP sign) up rough lane. At 'T-junction' turn L through gate and house yard to track beneath trees. On emerging keep straight on with hedge on R (obvious track). Pass L of line of hawthorns, then keep R of fence. From gate head L to farm. **③ ►** Enter farmyard and turn L between cowsheds, then immediately turn R to pass alongside barn to gate. Straight on, following hedge on R. **④ ►** Turn R through gate in this hedge and resume original direction to reach waymarked tree. Turn L and descend field to stile and footbridge. **⑤ ►** Climb alongside hedge/fence on L then bear R to stile at RH corner. Keep on uphill by hedge on L. After two more stiles bear R, and pass through gates to L of farm. **⑥ ►** Turn R and go up to next farm. Go between buildings and continue along tarmac lane. **⑦ ►** At first bend take stile up steps on R. Follow fence to stile, then cross depression towards fence stile. Don't cross it. Turn L through LH of two gateways and follow fence on R to stile. Bear L up next field, and when farm appears make for it. **⑧ ►** Pass through gates to L of farm and follow wall round to L. Turn R through gate opposite start of walled trackway. Head straight for house. **⑨ ►** Pass to R of house and straight on, following single power line towards RH of two prominent farms. **⑩ ►** Turn L along tarmac road and L again into Bay Gate Farm road. Bear R through farmyard to gate, then head L along field, through gateway in wall and contour round slope on L to wall stile. **⑪ ►** Turn R along road and L into tarmac lane (SP Harrop Fold ¾). **⑫ ►** Straight on through gate (wm) at end of hamlet onto cart track, through adjacent gates and head for barn. **⑬ ►** Through gate on R of barn and climb rough field to gap (wm) in wall at LH corner. Cross fence stile and turn L to follow path by wall. At end of trees turn R (wm) and descend by crumbling wall. **⑭ ►** At depression turn L into trackway going between walls. On reaching fence stile cross it to make detour to Beacon Hill (see note). Otherwise turn R and follow clear path near edge of wood. **⑮ ►** Turn R along road and take first roadside gate on L onto a broad green

Map labels

N

farm road

Harrop Gate
tip
Bay Gate Farm
⑩
Harrop Chapel
⑪
Tarmac lane
Harrop Fold
⑨
White Stones
⑫
road
Higher Heights Farm
⑧
Swan Barn
B
barn
⑮
⑬
road
Beacon Hill
A
⑤
FB
tree
⑯
wall
cleared forest
Shivering Ginnel
cleared forest
④
holly hedge
⑦
Till House
fence
⑭
Grindleton Plantation
⑥
don't cross it
⑰
hedge and tiny stream
farm
B
③
Hill House Farm
①
fence
line of hawthorns
awkward stile
A

two residents of Bay Gate

PARKING
Leave Grindleton by the Slaidburn road. Just out of the village, on the R, is a small layby by a 'Forest of Bowland' sign. Map ref: 757 464

Bus Turn Round
track under trees
② GRINDLETON
to Sawley, Gisburn
to Chatburn, Clitheroe

track. After passing through gap in wall, leave track and go alongside wall on L. Cross to other side of it and head up narrow field to stile at end. ⑯▶ Straight on through stile by gate and downhill over fence stile to another gate/stile. ⑰▶ Descend with hedge and tiny stream on R. Bear slightly L to ford stream coming down from L, and 50yds beyond it turn L to gate onto road. Turn R.

NOTE : DETOUR TO BEACON HILL No more than ½ a mile there and back, and strongly recommended, for it is a marvellous viewpoint. Cross fence stile and continue up track between walls to its end at a gate. The O.S. column (S 5159) is close by on the right.

Sika deer stag

Quiet walkers may catch a glimpse of the SIKA DEER, though it is a shy creature and keeps to the thick cover of the forest by day. The sika is not a native British deer; it was introduced into parks from Japan during the 17th.C., and is now established in the wild in this and a few other areas. In its spotted summer coat it resembles the slightly larger fallow deer. In winter the sika is plain and grey.

Many of GRINDLETON's houses were originally weavers' cottages, dating from the days when all cloth was produced on handlooms and transported by packhorse over the hills to market.

The tiny, secluded hamlet of HARROP FOLD has farmsteads of the early 17th.C. The lane thereto passes the delightful HARROP CHAPEL, standing, it seems, miles from anywhere. Built 1820-1, it is the oldest Methodist chapel in the area still in use. The adjoining cottage was, from 1850-74, a day school run by Mr. James Lord, and was known locally as 'Lord's Academy'.

Harrop Chapel

O.S. PATHFINDER (1 : 25 000) MAP
Nº 669 (S6 64/74) Clitheroe and Chipping

WALKS IN LANCASHIRE WITCH COUNTRY

11

THE ASCENT OF WEETS HILL
FROM BARNOLDSWICK
6 MILES

Weets Hill is the easternmost bulwark of the Pendle gritstone mass, for its tawny slopes sweep down into the light-green pastures of the West Craven limestone country. Though of modest altitude, the summit of Weets Hill is one of the finest viewpoints in Pendleside. A breezy, invigorating moorland ramble with gentle gradients.

J. Keighley

Lower Sandyford

ROUTE DIRECTIONS

① Go through stile by metal field gate on Barnoldswick side of bridge. Bear R up field (no path), heading towards small wood on skyline. Cross stile in fence and maintain direction to stile in corner. ② Turn R to climb steeply to slit stile in wall. Through it, then bear R through gap in walls and L over ladder-stile. Keep straight on up clear path to come alongside wall on L. ③ Turn L through stile (PW sign) in this wall and go forward along gravel track and lane. ④ Turn R along road, and when it forks keep L along Gillians Lane. ⑤ Turn L into Moorgate Road and keep straight on. It becomes a rough track, then regains a tarmac surface as it climbs steeply around two bends. ⑥ At fork keep R (straight on) along rough lane. ⑦ At far end of short concrete section take stile on R (PW sign) and turn L to continue uphill alongside lane. Go through gate/stile in crosswall and climb alongside wall on L. After crossing head of ravine look for path branching R to visit cairn and O.S. column beyond. ⑧ From summit bear L to return to wall, and follow it down to gate (PW sign). Pass to L of house and along tarmac lane. ⑨ Just before second house on L turn L through gate and up cart track. Through gate, turn L, through another gate and turn R. Follow wall to locate old cart track veering slightly L and follow it to gate/stile in crosswall. ⑩ Head for head! Pass through farmyard and go down farm road, staying with it as it turns R at next farm. ⑪ Turn L down rough, walled track. ⑫ Turn R along road. ⑬ At last house on L (Knowlden House) go through gate/stile (FP sign) and descend ½ L, keeping R of small barn, to stile at wall corner. Cross next field diagonally, aiming towards barn. There is a wall stile about 70 yds to R of it. ⑭ Go down alongside wall on L, and when it ends keep on down, bearing very slightly L, to stile just to L of tiny building. Straight on across next field to stile by metal gate, then head R along farm road. ⑮ Turn L down lane. Cross canal bridge, then turn L to follow canal towpath. A stile on R gives access to road at Park Bridge.

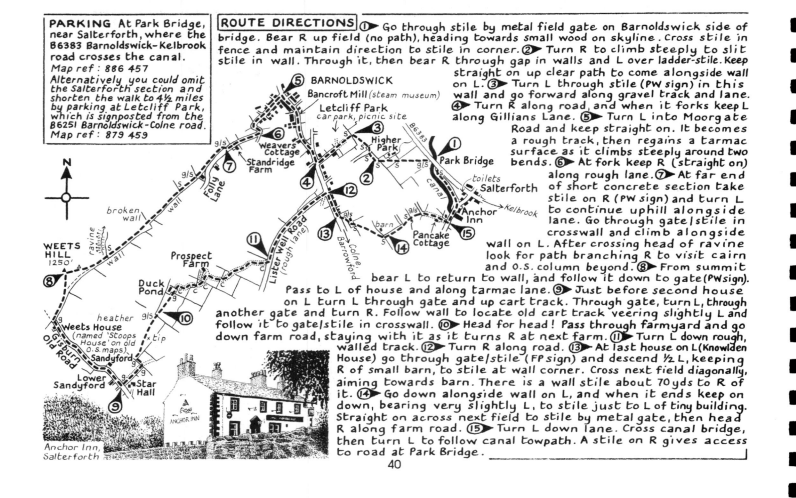

WEETS HILL 1250'

WEAVERS COTTAGE

BARNOLDSWICK
Bancroft Mill (steam museum)
Letcliff Park car park, picnic site

Higher Park

Park Bridge

toilets
Salterforth

Anchor Inn

Kelbrook

Pancake Cottage

Standridge Farm

Folly Lane

broken wall

Prospect Farm

Duck Pond

heather

Weets House (named 'Stoops House' on old O.S. maps)

Sandyford

Lower Sandyford

Star Hall

Gisburn Old Road

tip

Lister Well Road (rough lane)

Colne / Barrowford

barn

Anchor Inn, Salterforth

WELCOME TO BARNOLDSWICK

BARNOLDSWICK was a village as long ago as Saxon times. Recorded as 'Bernulfeswic' in the Domesday survey, it is now known to local folk as 'Barlick'. It is now a small town, and owes its growth to the coming of the canal and the textile industry. LETCLIFF PARK, a hillside garden with glorious views, was allowed to fall into a state of neglect, but is now being restored. BANCROFT MILL (1922) was the last cotton weaving shed to be built in Barlick. It closed in 1978 and was largely demolished, apart from the chimney and engine shed. The latter houses a 1915 steam engine in full working order, and is open to the public during the summer months.

MAKE SURE TO SELECT A CLEAR DAY, FOR WEETS HILL'S MAJOR VIRTUE IS AS A VIEWPOINT, WITH PARTICULARLY FINE PROSPECTS SOUTHWARDS TOWARDS PENDLE AND NORTHWARDS ACROSS CRAVEN TO THE 'THREE PEAKS'. THE LARGE CAIRN MARKS THE SITE OF A BEACON, LIT BY DENIZENS OF BARLICK TO CELEBRATE GREAT AND HISTORIC EVENTS (SUCH AS ROYAL JUBILEES AND CORONATIONS, OR BURNLEY F.C. WINNING A GAME).

The ANCHOR INN, a popular halt for canal tourists, has stalactites in the cellar caused by canal water seeping through the limestone walls.

The monstrous heads were fashioned in the 1980s by Peter Huby, art teacher and resident of Duck Pond

The bizarre statues of Duck Pond Farm

O.S. PATHFINDER (1:25 000) MAP
Nº 670 (SD 84/94) Barnoldswick and Earby

© Jack Keighley 1992

WALKS IN LANCASHIRE WITCH COUNTRY

12

THE LOST VALLEY OF THE TREACLE MINES

5¼ MILES

Since time immemorial the village of Sabden has been justly famous for its thriving treacle mining industry. Though the precise location of the mines is a closely guarded secret, this walk is nonetheless of rich historical interest.

Some superb Tudor farmsteads are visited on a circuit of a beautiful and secluded valley which has changed but little since witches trod its byways some 400 years ago.

Sabden Treacle Miners

J Keighley

Pendle Witch Inn, Sabden

ROUTE DIRECTIONS

① From car park entrance turn R to bridge and L into Stubbins Lane. ② Turn R along tarmac lane (with seats at end of it). When tarmac ends continue along rough lane. ③ 50 yds past cattle-grid turn R off track and head slightly L towards farm on hillside. Locate footbridge to cross stream, then go straight up field to gate on R of farm. ④ Cross facing wall stile, then turn L and follow wall past farm. When wall bends L a clear path goes straight on up hillside. When it peters out keep on up to stile in top LH corner of field. Turn L along tarmac lane. ⑤ Just past Borough of Pendle sign take step-stile L, then turn R to another step stile in crosswall. Thin path goes forward to reach cart-track. Go L down it. ⑥ When cart-track turns L leave it and go R of wall corner to cross step-stile. Turn R and follow wall to next farm. ⑦ Turn R up drive for 60 yds then L onto path (signposted) between fences and down to stile. Turn R to gate at wall corner and continue alongside wall on L. ⑧ Look for step-stile (easily missed) in wall on L. Head R to another step-stile, then follow fence on L to next farm. ⑨ At farmyard turn L to gate into muddy track. When it ends, keep on forward over concrete bridge to gate L of house. Continue along farm road. ⑩ Keep R at road junction. When road turns R go straight forward, to R of small stream, to stile. Ford stream and go up to gate on L. Pass through it and follow wall on L. ⑪ When wall on L ends keep straight on across next field to stile near RH corner, then head for ruined house. ⑫ At ruin turn L to rising farm road. Follow it to next farm. ⑬ Don't enter farmyard. Turn R off farm road and follow wall on L. Turn R alongside plantation, and go on beyond end of it to a point where a path comes down moor from R. Here turn sharp L and follow stream down to a small gate. Continue L along reservoir road. ⑭ When plantation on L ends go through small gate on L. Follow railings past a small building, then turn R to a small metal gate. Follow fence on L and descend to farm. Turn L through yard to tarmac lane. ⑮ Turn R down lane. At fork keep L and at next keep R to visit church.

PARKING

At Sabden. Car park in the village centre, opposite the White Hart Inn.
Map ref: 779 374

The 16-acre reservoir is a fly fishery stocked with brown and rainbow trout.

slopes of Spence Moor

Cock Clough Plantation

Churn Clough Reservoir ⑭

Wood House Brook

⑬ Stainscomb

Sabden Fold

ruin

modern barn

Ratten Clough Farm

vaccary walling

ruin

⑫

⑪

⑩

The Old House

concrete slab

New York Farm ⑮

Heyhouses

fence

⑨ Lower Houses

FOR NOTES ON SABDEN SEE WALK 3

② ③

SABDEN

caravans

Dean Farm

⑥ Back o' th' Hill

⑧

to Clitheroe toilets

Sabden Brook

FB

trees

Borough of Pendle sign

Padiham Heights ⑦

① car park

to Read and padham

Dry Corner Farm ④

⑤ tarmac lane

to Whalley

TREACLE MINING

At a secret location on the slopes of Pendle, and carefully concealed by tall black pudding trees, are the entrances to the deep mine which yields the raw treacle rock. This ore is locally melted down, refined and processed to produce the unique Sabden Treacle, most of which is then woven into parkin. Any treacle of inferior quality, however, is sent to a Preston flypaper manufacturer. Those interested in learning more of the history of this complex industry and the fascinating characters involved are recommended to visit the Treacle Mining Exhibition, which is just along the path from the car park. Open daily, admission free. Children will be enchanted.

Stainscomb

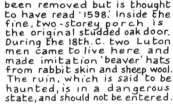

In front of a huge, bracken-clad hollow in the flank of Spence Moor stands this gaunt and melancholy ruin of a once-noble Tudor farmstead. The datestone has been removed but is thought to have read '1598.' Inside the fine, two-storey porch is the original studded oak door. During the 18th. C. two Luton men came to live here and made imitation 'beaver' hats from rabbit skin and sheep wool. The ruin, which is said to be haunted, is in a dangerous state, and should not be entered.

Another house of the same vintage, but well-preserved and occupied, is LOWER HOUSES. Small diamonds of stained glass in the lower right-hand windows are said to have come from Whalley Abbey.

● BETWEEN STAINSCOMB AND RATTEN CLOUGH IS A STRETCH OF WALL CONSTRUCTED OF UPRIGHT STONE SLABS. THIS IS KNOWN AS 'VACCARY WALLING'. (See Walk 4).

The row of cottages by the brook at HEYHOUSES was the scene of a chapter in Harrison Ainsworth's 'The Lancashire Witches.'

O.S. PATHFINDER (1 : 25 000) MAPS
Nº 680 (SD 63/73) Longridge and Great Harwood
Nº 681 (SD 83/93) Burnley

© Jack Keighley 1992

43

WALKS IN LANCASHIRE WITCH COUNTRY

13

LIMESTONE LANDSCAPES

4½ MILES

A short walk around Worsaw Hill, the most prominent of a number of smooth, rounded limestone knolls which characterise the lovely Downham countryside. Don't expect to find spectacular scars, pavements and potholes like those of the Yorkshire Dales; this is a gentle stroll through rich, emerald-green farmland. Ideal for a hot summer's day.

stile near Worsaw End

packhorse bridge, Smithies Brook

PARKING Car park and toilets at lower end of Downham village, near the bridge.
Map ref: 784 441

FOR NOTES ON DOWNHAM SEE WALK 2

Map labels:
Smithies Brook
packhorse bridge
FB
Downham Bridge
Sunken track blocked by fallen trees. Walk alongside it
barn
concrete posts
9
8
barn
farm
railway
mind the nettles
copse
CHATBURN
A59
line of Roman road
11
toilets
to Downham
7
line of Roman road
toilets
DOWNHAM
6
White Croft Wood
car park
1
run for your life
5
Longlands Wood
Piked Acre Wood
N
Warren Hill
Worsaw Hill 725'
2
line of trees
4
mound
3
barn
Worsaw End (farm)

ROUTE DIRECTIONS
① From car park entrance turn R up farm road to stile by gate. Follow green tractor trail, with fence/hedge on R. ② After crossing a stile keep straight on (no path), passing RH end of line of trees to reach stone stile in corner. ③ Cross bottom of next field to another stone stile. To ascend Worsaw Hill from here, take a path (faint at first) slanting up the hillside. It's not an official right-of-way, but is well-used. Otherwise, from stile, continue along foot of slope with wall on L. ④ Bear slightly R away from wall. Pass between outcrops and follow thin path to stile in fence. Descend by wall to ladder-stile, then straight across next field to stile onto A 59. ⑤ Cross road and go down V-shaped path to turn R over stile. Pass to R of long, low building and through trees to stile in old lane. Take facing stile to continue forward, then veer R to cross track, up to R of Methodist church and forward to road. ⑥ (Detour L to visit Chatburn). Turn R to follow road out of village. ⑦ Cross high bridge over A59 then turn L through gate/stile (public footpath sign). Go down by fence on L and bear R to follow field boundary to stile into enclosed, overgrown track. Cross railway bridge and stay with track until it peters out, then keep straight on. ⑧ Just before reaching barn turn R through gate set at an angle. Go through gate at far end of barn, then turn R to follow wall, eventually descending to small footbridge. ⑨ Cross FB and turn R across field to gateway and path into trees. Go up by RH side of wood to road. ⑩ Turn R along road. ⑪ Just past a small copse on the L, turn L through stone stile. Climb gently towards wood. Turn L alongside wood, through stile and down by wall to road. Turn R into Downham and L at road junction.

This is an area particularly rich in wildlife. There are rabbits and pheasants everywhere. Hares and foxes are common, and deer are sometimes seen – mostly sika (see Walk 10). Birdsong fills the air, and the botanist will find much of interest. As in all limestone areas, there are snails in profusion.

44

REEF KNOLLS are smooth, rounded hillocks of almost pure limestone. Some 300 million years ago, during the geological era known as the Carboniferous period, this area lay submerged beneath a shallow sea. Bodies of myriads of dead sea-creatures were swept by water currents into submarine ridges. In later geological times earth movements lifted these mounds of limestone above the level of the sea. Often they are quarried, but WORSAW HILL is safe, having been declared an S.S.S.I. (Site of Special Scientific Interest). The tiny shells and skeletons which formed the limestone can be clearly seen in the walls around the base of the hill.

CHATBURN

is thought to have taken its name from St. Ceatt or Chad. It is a large village, and is more industrialised than others in the district, though its once-thriving textile industry has now dwindled to just one surviving mill. Limestone quarrying and the production of road-surfacing materials are important local industries. Prominent in the village centre is Hudson's Ice Cream Shop; this building was originally a toll house on the 18th.C. Clitheroe-Skipton turnpike road.

 The railway reached Chatburn in 1850, and was extended to Hellifield in the 1870s. The line closed to regular passenger services on 10 September 1962, but still has occasional trains.

 The A59 Clitheroe By-pass opened on New Year's Day 1971.

O.S. PATHFINDER (1 : 25 000) MAP
Nº 669 (SD 64/74) Clitheroe and Chipping

© Jack Keighley 1992

45

14

SALLEY ABBEY & THE RIBBLE GORGE

5¾ MILES

The tranquil ruins of a small Cistercian abbey, a low wooded ridge with exquisite views across to Pendle, and a glorious riverside path are the ingredients which make up this delectable ramble. The walk, however, involves two death-defying crossings of the racetrack known as the A59(T). An ability to sprint to Olympic Games standard is an advantage.

Salley Abbey and Pendle

ROUTE DIRECTIONS

① At rear of car park opposite Spread Eagle are two stiles. Take the RH one and bear R across field (aim for steep end of Pendle). Go over wall stile and straight on to stile into farm lane. **②** Cross lane to overgrown track up through trees. Pass R of wood to ladder-stile and up to A59. Cross to facing stile and turn L along farm road. Follow it through farmyard and keep straight on up road to Higher Greenhead Farm. Straight through farmyard and into field. **③** Go up field, aiming slightly to R of distant plantation. Through gate and keep to RH side of next field to stile in corner. Straight on, passing L of barn. **④** Just past barn take stile on L into plantation. Keep near LH side of wood to stile at its far end. Forward, with fence on L, through two fields. **⑤** About 60 yds from end of second field cross fence to farm road. Straight through farmyard to big iron gate and follow power lines down to railway. **⑥** Cross track to facing gate and follow hedge on R up to Great Dudland. Head L along drive. **⑦** Turn R along main road and in 100 yds take stile in hedge on L. Follow hedge on L to gate. Continue forward with hedge on R, then bear L past barn. **⑧** Turn R along rough lane. **⑨** Just before reaching farm turn L through gate. Cross railway bridge and follow fence/hedge on L to next farmyard, from where turn L along farm road.

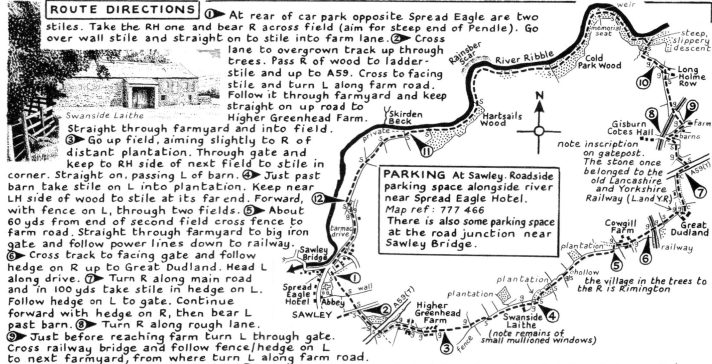

Swanside Laithe

PARKING
At Sawley. Roadside parking space alongside river near Spread Eagle Hotel. Map ref : 777 466 There is also some parking space at the road junction near Sawley Bridge.

note inscription on gatepost. The stone once belonged to the old Lancashire and Yorkshire Railway (L.and Y.R.)

the village in the trees to the R is Rimington

(note remains of small mullioned windows)

⑩ When farm road bends L, take gate (wm) on R. Follow hedge on R down to depression, where turn R over stile (wm). Follow fence to ladder-stile into wood. Path descends very gradually at first, then turns sharp L and zig-zags steeply down to river. Turn L on clear riverside path (Ribble Way). **⑪** Look for a ladder-stile slightly up to L. Follow fence to cross two more ladder-stiles and continue forward with fence on L. **⑫** Go L through stile, footbridge and gate, then turn R to pass through gates to tarmac drive back to Sawley.

SLOW! FREE RANGE CHILDREN
sign at Higher Greenhead Farm

SALLEY ABBEY

'Salley' (from sallow, a type of willow) is the abbey's original name, though it is better known as 'Sawley'. This small daughter house of Fountains was founded in 1147. It was never wealthy, and much of the stonework of the fragmentary ruins is crudely shaped and of poor quality. There were 21 monks in residence at the Dissolution, and the last abbot, William Trafford, having taken part in the 'Pilgrimage of Grace', was executed for treason on 10th. March 1537. The abbey is open daily (except Mondays) from 10a.m. Admission free.

Gisburn Cotes Hall

Note at GREAT DUDLAND the old cheese-press by the wall and, in front of the house, a stone coffin from Salley Abbey.
GISBURN COTES HALL has a 1659 datestone above the porch door.

The most beautiful section of the RIBBLE WAY is that between Gisburn and Sawley, where the river flows through a deeply-cut, wooded valley. RAINSBER SCAR, a high limestone cliff at a bend of the river, is known as PUDSAY'S LEAP. Sir William Pudsay, in the 16th.C., made his own money from silver obtained from a mine on his estate at Rimington. He was found out, and it is said that in fleeing from his pursuers he leapt his horse down the Scar and over the Ribble. He escaped uninjured and was eventually pardoned by Queen Elizabeth I.

The railway was built by the LANCASHIRE and YORKSHIRE RAILWAY Co. (completed 1880). A typical L.Y.R. locomotive was this 2-4-2T, designed by Sir John Aspinall and built in the 1890s.

O.S. PATHFINDER (1:25000) MAPS
Nº 669 (SD 64/74) Clitheroe and Chipping
Nº 670 (SD 84/94) Barnoldswick and Earby

© Jack Keighley 1992

47

15

GREAT EDGE & NOYNA ROCKS

6 MILES

Canal Wharf at Foulridge, an absorbing place for students of industrial archaeology, makes an interesting starting-point for this pleasant excursion into the upland country of the Lancs/Yorks border. Careful reference to map and/or route directions is required in order not to go astray on this rather complex route with its many twists and turns.

Noyna End Farm
J Keighley

ROUTE DIRECTIONS ① Walk back to wharf entrance and straight on up tarmac road. ② Turn L along Town Gate, cross green and up steps to main road. Turn R. ③ Turn L opposite 'Causeway' and R at New Inn. ④ In a few yards turn L up rough lane between walls. At end of walled section keep straight on uphill. ⑤ When track bends L go straight on through gated stile and line of stiles. ⑥ Turn L alongside wire fence. In 120 yds turn R over stile and head straight across field (reservoir is ahead and slightly to R). After two gates a cart track develops. ⑦ Just before reaching farm bear ½ L across field to wooden stile at bend of farm road. Follow farm road forward across reservoir. ⑧ Just past bungalow turn L through stone stile by gate and follow clear path down past end of reservoir to farm. ⑨ Don't enter farmyard. Look to the R and you will see two gated stiles. Take the one nearer to the farm, then bear L down to stile and slab bridge. Cross it and keep R up alongside tiny stream. In 100 yds cross stile and follow clear path bearing R through stiles to Moss Houses. ⑩ Bear L through farmyard and along farm road, bearing R at white house. Keep straight on at Y-junction. ⑪ On reaching ford cross slab bridge to stile and turn L across field to another stile. Straight across golf course (don't walk on greens) to wall stile (partially blocked to keep sheep off course), then head for farm. ⑫ Pass to L of buildings and straight on, with wall on L, to next farm. Turn R down farm road and L along lane. ⑬ In 300 yds take metal field-gate on L and climb hillside (see note below map) to derelict farm. Pass to R of all buildings, through gap and turn R to follow wall to stile. Cross rough field to next stile, but don't use it. ⑭ Turn sharp L and climb to top of moor. Turn L at wall and descend along crest of ridge. ⑮ Turn R (PW sign) and follow clear path to footbridge. Up far bank to green track and turn L. Turn R up lane and in 10 yds go L through gap by end of wall. Follow wall on L. ⑯ Go L over wooden stile at angle of wall, then turn R and head towards sloping Noyna Rocks. ⑰ Turn R and climb to ladder-stile at LH corner of field. Turn L. Pass round wall corner, through stile and continue with wall on L. ⑱ Turn L through step stile and forward, keeping R of quarry to follow green path through gateway in wall. 50 yds past gateway fork R on thinner path. Cross wall stile on R by hollies and follow wall down to road. Turn L. ⑲ Turn R into Cragg Farm and immediately sharp L through metal gate to follow wall on R round to road. ⑳ Go through facing stile and bear

Daubers Bridge • FB • dismantled railway • kiln car park • ② ⑳ ⑲ ⑱ • Noyna Hill • ⑯ • FB • Great Edge • quarry • ⑭ • quarry fence • quarry • Flass Bent • Canal Wharf • shop • A56 • FOULRIDGE • quarry • Noyna Rocks • Noyna End • ⑰ • ⑮ • Flass Bent Well (derelict farm) • Flass Bent • New Inn • B6251 • tunnel • ② ③ ④ ⑤ ⑥ • Lower Broach Farm • fence • tiny stream • hopefully • ① Canal Wharf

N (compass)

Sorry – no space for a picture on this page.

⑩ ⑪ • New House • Far Salter Syke • ⑬ • Moss Houses • Colne Golf Club • ⑫ Near Salter Syke • farm • ⑦ • Lower Clough • Foulridge Upper Reservoir • ⑧ • ⑨

PARKING AT Canal Wharf, signposted from A56 at Foulridge. Car park just beyond the old railway bridge.
Map ref: 888 427

NOTE: Points ⑬ to ⑭. When the walk was researched (Nov 91) the gates marked * were securely tied and had to be climbed. The farmer, however, has kindly promised to make his gates openable and provide a stile as shown.

R down to sunken track at field corner. Cross disused railway and keep straight on to reach footbridge. Bear slightly L to canal bridge and turn L along towpath.

CANAL WHARF

originally received and despatched cotton, coal and other goods coming to and from Colne by canal transport. Now the wharf is used entirely for recreation. The leisure cruiser 'Marton Emperor' takes sightseers through the famous Foulridge Tunnel, which is dead straight, nearly a mile long and took five years to build (opened 1796). It has no internal towpath, and 'leggers' had to lie on planks fixed to the barges and 'walk' along the tunnel wall, pushing the barge with them. In 1912 a cow fell into the canal and swam through the tunnel to Foulridge, where it was rescued and revived with alcohol from the Hole in the Wall pub! Near the car park is a re-constructed kiln. The railway closed in 1970. Refreshments are available from the shop which occupies the former stables.

STABLE SHOP & TEA GARDEN
TEA · COFFEE · SNACKS · GIFTS · PROVISIONS · SOUVENIRS

The two large RESERVOIRS at Foulridge were built to provide a supply of water into the summit level of the Leeds/Liverpool Canal. The lower reservoir is also known as LAKE BURWAIN. Both support a large variety of waterfowl. NOYNA ROCKS has long been a favourite picnic place for local families, and children in particular take great delight in scrambling over the gently sloping slabs of millstone grit.

O.S. PATHFINDER (1:25 000) MAP
Nº 670 (SD 84/94) Barnoldswick and Earby

© Jack Keighley 1992

49

THE ASCENT OF PENDLE HILL

FROM BARLEY via BOAR CLOUGH

5 MILES

A great walk with a real 'witch country flavour', where one will experience the full impact of Pendle's wild, brooding grandeur. For all but the first half-mile the route coincides with the Pendle Way, and is well-waymarked. Wonderful views and varied landscapes. Be sure to take a compass in case it's misty, and binoculars in case it isn't.

Lower Ogden Reservoir

ROUTE DIRECTIONS

① From car park entrance turn R and go up lane to R of Village Hall. Stay with main track past lower reservoir and on up the valley. ② Ignore farm road going up to R. Keep L on lower path to upper reservoir dam. ③ Climb to R of dam and continue alongside reservoir on path between wall and fence. Cross stile and continue on clear path up valley to ladder-stile. ④ From ladder-stile take broad upper path. Cross stream (Boar Clough). ⑤ Follow clear path with 'Pendle Way' signs, at first high above the clough but gradually descending to reach stream level. ⑥ Cross stream and continue alongside it for about 200 yds, then, at a waymark, bear R to leave gully and follow a line of cairns. At a large cairn turn L and head northwards to reach the O.S. column at the summit. ⑦ Continue northwards. Just before coming to a crosswall turn sharp R to descend 'constructed' path. ⑧ At farm road turn R and pass along front of Pendle House to gate/stile at far end of buildings. ⑨ Turn L and follow wall down. Through gate then bear slightly R, through gully and over stile on R. Pass L of house to kissing-gate(wm) ⑩ Follow obvious path near stream down to Ings End. ⑪ Turn R along tarmac lane. ⑫ When lane bends L cross footbridge on R. Turn L past the end of a wall and follow stream down into Barley. Turn R along main street, and at bus station take path between road and stream.

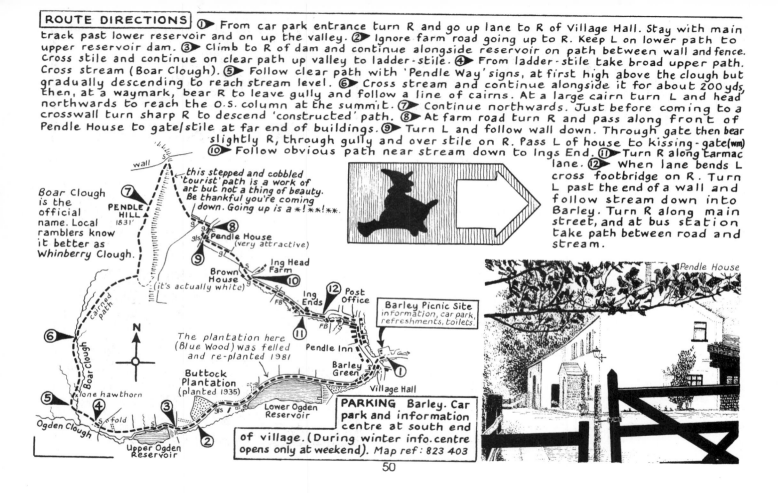

Boar Clough is the official name. Local ramblers know it better as Whinberry Clough.

this stepped and cobbled 'tourist' path is a work of art but not a thing of beauty. Be thankful you're coming down. Going up is a *!**!**.

PENDLE HILL 1831'

Pendle House (very attractive)

Ing Head Farm

Brown House (it's actually white)

cairned path

Ing Ends

Post Office

Pendle Inn

Barley Green

Village Hall

The plantation here (Blue Wood) was felled and re-planted 1981

Buttock Plantation (planted 1935)

lone hawthorn

fold

Ogden Clough

Upper Ogden Reservoir

Lower Ogden Reservoir

Barley Picnic Site information, car park, refreshments, toilets.

PARKING Barley. Car park and information centre at south end of village. (During winter info. centre opens only at weekend). Map ref: 823 403

Pendle House

wall

N

BARLEY

The Barley Mow Restaurant

This small, attractive village is highly popular with ramblers and tourists. It began life as a 13th.C. vaccary, and was called *Barelegh* (infertile lea or meadow). Barley has always been a farming community, but in the last century there were two cotton mills here — at Barley Green and Narrow-gates. The former, which is passed on this walk, was wrecked by floods in the 1880s, and is now a N.W.W.A. filter station.

OGDEN RESERVOIRS

LOWER RESERVOIR
Completed : 1914
Area : 21·12 acres
Max depth : 59 feet
Capacity : 157·5 million gallons

UPPER RESERVOIR
Completed : 1906
Area : 7·01 acres
Max depth : 58 feet
Capacity : 54·5 million gallons

Drinking water for the Nelson area.

O.S. PATHFINDER (1:25 000) MAPS
At the 1:25 000 scale Pendle Hill has 'edge-of-map' problems, for 4 sheets meet at a point close to the summit. This route passes through all 4, as shown in the diagram below.

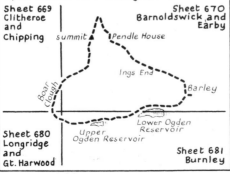

Sheet 669 Clitheroe and Chipping

Sheet 670 Barnoldswick and Earby

summit — Pendle House

Ings End

Boar Clough

Barley

Upper Ogden Reservoir

Lower Ogden Reservoir

Sheet 680 Longridge and Gt. Harwood

Sheet 681 Burnley

© Jack Keighley 1992

51

17

WADDINGTON

6 MILES

A visit to Waddington is an absolute *must*. Steeped in history and tended with pride by its residents, this gem of a village is undoubtedly one of the prettiest in Lancashire. An easy and peaceful walk through lush, green, gently sloping pastures at the very heart of the Ribble Valley, with a satisfying finish along the riverbank.

Waddington Parish Church

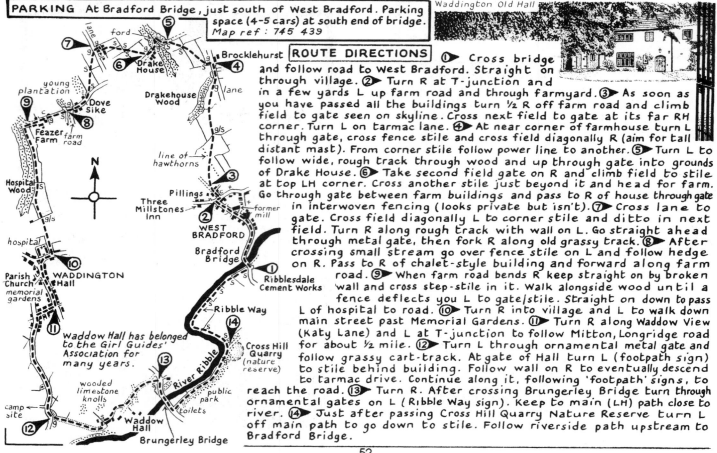

PARKING At Bradford Bridge, just south of West Bradford. Parking space (4–5 cars) at south end of bridge. Map ref: 745 439

Waddington Old Hall

ROUTE DIRECTIONS

① Cross bridge and follow road to West Bradford. Straight on through village. ② Turn R at T-junction and in a few yards L up farm road and through farmyard. ③ As soon as you have passed all the buildings turn ½ R off farm road and climb field to gate seen on skyline. Cross next field to gate at its far RH corner. Turn L on tarmac lane. ④ At near corner of farmhouse turn L through gate, cross fence stile and cross field diagonally R (aim for tall distant mast). From corner stile follow power line to another. ⑤ Turn L to follow wide, rough track through wood and up through gate into grounds of Drake House. ⑥ Take second field gate on R and climb field to stile at top LH corner. Cross another stile just beyond it and head for farm. Go through gate between farm buildings and pass to R of house through gate in interwoven fencing (looks private but isn't). ⑦ Cross lane to gate. Cross field diagonally L to corner stile and ditto in next field. Turn R along rough track with wall on L. Go straight ahead through metal gate, then fork R along old grassy track. ⑧ After crossing small stream go over fence stile on L and follow hedge on R. Pass to R of chalet-style building and forward along farm road. ⑨ When farm road bends R keep straight on by broken wall and cross step-stile in it. Walk alongside wood until a fence deflects you L to gate/stile. Straight on down to pass L of hospital to road. ⑩ Turn R into village and L to walk down main street past Memorial Gardens. ⑪ Turn R along Waddow View (Katy Lane) and L at T-junction to follow Mitton, Longridge road for about ½ mile. ⑫ Turn L through ornamental metal gate and follow grassy cart-track. At gate of Hall turn L (footpath sign) to stile behind building. Follow wall on R to eventually descend to tarmac drive. Continue along it, following 'footpath' signs, to reach the road. ⑬ Turn R. After crossing Brungerley Bridge turn through ornamental gates on L (Ribble Way sign). Keep to main (LH) path close to river. ⑭ Just after passing Cross Hill Quarry Nature Reserve turn L off main path to go down to stile. Follow riverside path upstream to Bradford Bridge.

Waddow Hall has belonged to the Girl Guides' Association for many years.

WEST BRADFORD, a pleasant village with a long history, has grown considerably in recent years as a result of much residential development. The old cotton mill, Riverside Mill, is being converted into houses, cottages and apartments.

WADDINGTON

Arms of the Waddington family

A chuckling stream bisects this delightful village, which is dominated by the 18thC tower of St. Helen's Church. St. Helen is said to have been a British princess and mother of Constantine the Great. The church (apart from the tower) was rebuilt 1824-8 and again, in early Perpendicular style, 1898-1901. The West Window depicts St. Helen, King Henry VI and Wada, an Anglo-Saxon chieftain after whom the village is named. Near the church is an old pinfold (pound for stray animals) and the village stocks. At the top of the village are the almshouses known as the 'Widows' Hospital'. They were built in 1700 (the gateway is original). Later they were rebuilt and grouped around a green with a small chapel.

Following his defeat at the Battle of Hexham in 1464, during the Wars of the Roses, Lancastrian KING HENRY VI found refuge first at Bolton Hall and then at Waddington Hall. However, his presence at Waddington was discovered by the Yorkists, and in attempting to flee he was captured at the stepping-stones at Brungerley (where the bridge now stands).

Henry VI

O.S. PATHFINDER (1:25 000) MAP
Nº 669 (SD 64/74) Clitheroe and Chipping

© Jack Keighley 1992

18

THE LEAFY LANES OF RIMINGTON

5½ MILES

Nestling among the folds of the undulating limestone country to the north of Pendle lie a host of tranquil villages and tiny hamlets linked by a complex network of narrow, leafy lanes. This is excellent rambling country, best sampled during late spring and summer when birdsong fills the air and the hedgerows are bedecked with flowers.

Rimington

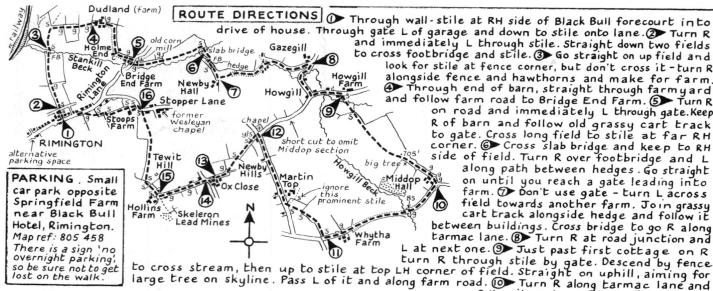

ROUTE DIRECTIONS

① Through wall-stile at RH side of Black Bull forecourt into drive of house. Through gate L of garage and down to stile onto lane. **②** Turn R and immediately L through stile. Straight down two fields to cross footbridge and stile. **③** Go straight on up field and look for stile at fence corner, but don't cross it - turn R alongside fence and hawthorns and make for farm. **④** Through end of barn, straight through farmyard and follow farm road to Bridge End Farm. **⑤** Turn R on road and immediately L through gate. Keep R of barn and follow old grassy cart track to gate. Cross long field to stile at far RH corner. **⑥** Cross slab bridge and keep to RH side of field. Turn R over footbridge and L along path between hedges. Go straight on until you reach a gate leading into farm. **⑦** Don't use gate - turn L across field towards another farm. Join grassy cart track alongside hedge and follow it between buildings. Cross bridge to go R along tarmac lane. **⑧** Turn R at road junction and L at next one. **⑨** Just past first cottage on R turn R through stile by gate. Descend by fence to cross stream, then up to stile at top LH corner of field. Straight on uphill, aiming for large tree on skyline. Pass L of it and along farm road. **⑩** Turn R along tarmac lane and follow it past next farm. **⑪** Almost at end of lane go R over wall-stile and follow fence/hedge on L to another. Straight across field to gate/stile (L of farm) then go R down lane to chapel. **⑫** Take stile on L (FP Ox Close ¼), and follow fence on L. When fence bends R cross stile in it and go diagonally (aim for Pendle) across field, through gate and along farm road. **⑬** Turn L through farmyard, R between buildings and R down tarmac lane. **⑭** Take farm road to L of house called 'Woodlands'. **⑮** Just before reaching farm take stile

PARKING

Small car park opposite Springfield Farm near Black Bull Hotel, Rimington. Map ref: 805 458 There is a sign 'no overnight parking', so be sure not to get lost on the walk.

Rimington.

1. Je - sus shall reign where-e'er the sun Doth his suc-ces-sive jour-neys run;

Hymn tune. composer FRANCIS DUCKWORTH lived at Rimington and attended the chapel at Stopper Lane. He named his best-known tune after the village, and 'Rimington' is known the world over where people sing 'Jesus Shall Reign'. The chapel is now a private house with a commemorative plaque.

54

on R. Go up RH side of field, over stile and in 60yds turn R over fence stile. Straight on, with fence on L, then descend to stile on L of large garage. ⑯ ➤ Go L along road. Just past farm take stile on L (FP Rimington ¼). Straight on over fence stile. At end of next field cross stile on R, turn L to corner stile and bear R to gate.

Rimington

A small, linear village, peaceful and pretty, and of sufficient antiquity to have been mentioned in the Domesday Book. Many of the farms and barns at Rimington have in recent years been tastefully converted into very desirable private residences. There is a pub but no church, and the only shop(*) is, somewhat incongruously, a high-class fashion house. The author, having spent his childhood here (at the house called 'Fern Lea'), has a special affection for this walk, for all these fields and woods, lanes and streams were his idyllic playground.

* There is a small Post Office and General Store at nearby Stopper Lane.

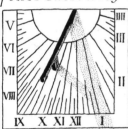

flies swift away

V · IIII · III · II · VI · VII · VIII · IX · X · XI · XII · I

sundial on the wall of the chapel at Martin Top.

Stoops Farm, Stopper Lane

MIDDOP HALL is a fine 16th C. farmhouse. High in the front wall of the barn can be seen a fragment of masonry from Salley Abbey. It was from the SKELERON LEAD MINES that Sir William Pudsay obtained the silver for his counterfeit shillings (see Walk 14).

O.S. PATHFINDER (1:25 000) MAP
Nº670 (SD 84/94) Barnoldswick and Earby

© Jack Keighley 1992

19

A CANALSIDE WALK IN CRAVEN

5¾ MILES

A most unusual and interesting walk of extreme contrasts. From Greenberfield, the 'summit' of the Leeds/Liverpool Canal, there are lovely views across the hummocky limestone landscapes of West Craven. Two beautiful old churches and a charming village will be admired before we conclude the walk by following the towpath as it winds fascinatingly between dark, Satanic mills.

Penkle Witch

J Keighley

Greenberfield

PARKING Car park and picnic area at Greenberfield Bridge, Greenberfield Lane, off the B6252 Barnoldswick-Thornton-in-Craven road.
Map ref: 888 482

For notes on Barnoldswick see Walk II

St. Mary's, Thornton-in-Craven

ROUTE DIRECTIONS ① From car park walk up to canal and turn L along towpath, passing under road bridge. ② Cross next bridge (PW signs) to resume towpath walk. ③ Just around LH bend of canal take wall stile (PW sign) on R. Walk alongside high fence, with factory on L, to gate/stile, then turn L and follow fence/wall to road. ④ Turn L along road. Almost opposite main gates of factory go through kissing-gate (PW sign) on R and ascend clear path to stile into churchyard. ⑤ Go through churchyard to leave by church gate. Turn L and L again to go down walled track to old stone bridge. Keep straight on across golf course, passing L of plantation and through plantation beyond (PW sign) to metal kissing-gate. Keep straight on over shoulder of hill and head for church. ⑥ Turn R along road. ⑦ At main road detour L to visit village, then return to junction and continue along main road. ⑧ Where road bends L (County of North Yorkshire sign) go through gate on R (PW sign). Follow fence on L (ignore PW stile in it) to gate at field corner. Keep straight on through gate/stile in crosswall, and straight on across the next field, at the far side of which there is a stile made partly of wood and partly of stone. ⑨ Straight on, heading for large tree on skyline. 25 yds to R of it is a fence stile. ⑩ Keep to RH side of field to reach stone stile by gate, then head past metal power-line post to farm. Go straight through farmyard and along farm road. ⑪ Cross lane to facing stile and straight ahead (clear path) down field. Halfway down field bear slightly L to follow wall down to canal bridge. ⑫ Don't cross bridge unless you wish to visit Canal Shop. Turn R along towpath. ⑬ At next bridge (No 153) cross canal to resume towpath walk - about a mile to Greenberfield.

THIS IS THE EASIEST WALK IN THE BOOK.

British Waterways

The 127-mile-long LEEDS and LIVERPOOL CANAL opened in 1816 and brought prosperity to places like Barnoldswick. Raw cotton for the textile industry came up from Liverpool, and the canal also transported limestone, coal and other vital supplies. The original 3-flight lock-staircase at GREENBERFIELD, which raised the canal to its summit level of 487', was replaced by 3 single locks in 1820. This project necessitated a slight change in the line of the canal, and the pre-1820 route is clearly visible on the left as we begin the walk.

GILL HALL, a 16th C house, was once used as a rectory. The lovely church of ST. MARY-LE-GHYLL (or le-Gill or the Gill) is so named because it stands at the edge of a ravine. Cistercian monks from Fountains came to Barlick in 1147 to attempt to establish a monastery, but various adversities forced them, within 5 years, to move to a new site at Kirkstall, Leeds. Monks returned from Kirkstall (c1160) to build the first Gill Church. The massive tower was added in the 16th C (dated MCCCCCXXIIII). The interior has many ancient features, including superb Jacobean box-pews and a 3-decker pulpit with overhead sounding-board. Alongside the porch is a stone coffin said to have held the remains of a monk who died whilst the church was being built. A little tearoom by the church gate is open from 2-5 Sat. and Sun. from April to September.
ST. MARY'S, THORNTON largely dates from the 15th C. In the churchyard is an octagonal well-house bearing the date MDCCLXIV.

St. Mary-le-Ghyll, Barnoldswick

O.S. PATHFINDER (1:25 000) MAP
Nº 681 (SD 83/93) Burnley

© Jack Keighley 1992

NICK O' PENDLE FROM WISWELL

5¾ MILES

This bracing walk, with extensive and ever-changing views, takes us from wooded limestone hills to the bleak gritstone of Pendle's western slopes. Much of the walk is on potentially muddy farm tracks, so ideally it should be done during a dry summer spell. Hot and weary wayfarers will relish the sublime prospect of a pint at the midway – and highest – point.

cottages at Wiswell   J. Keighley

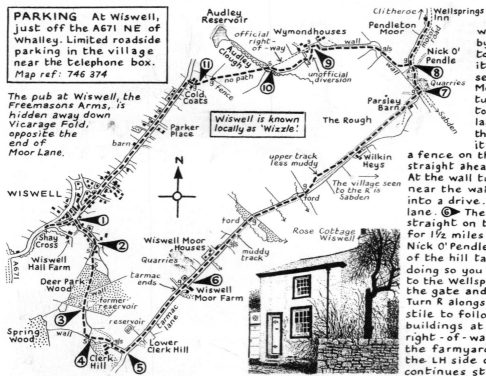

The pub at Wiswell, the Freemasons Arms, is hidden away down Vicarage Fold, opposite the end of Moor Lane.

Wiswell is known locally as 'Wizzle'!

Audley Reservoir

official right-of-way

Wymondhouses

Clitheroe↑ | Wellsprings Inn

Pendleton Moor

wall

motor road

Nick O' Pendle

Audley Clough

no path

unofficial diversion

Quarries

Cold Coats

fence

Parsley Barn

Sabden

Parker Place

The Rough

barn

WISWELL

N

upper track less muddy

Wilkin Heys

The village seen to the R is Sabden

ford

Shay Cross

Wiswell Hall Farm

Wiswell Moor Houses

Quarries

ford

Rose Cottage Wiswell

A671

Deer Park Wood

tarmac ends

muddy track

former reservoir

reservoir

tarmac lane

Wiswell Moor Farm

Spring Wood

wall

Clerk Hill

Lower Clerk Hill

ROUTE DIRECTIONS

① Walk west out of the village (towards the by-pass) to see the Shay Cross. Return to the village and have a potter around its various lanes and alleys before setting off, from the telephone box, up Moor Lane. ② Just past Manor Cottage turn R through a gate (FP sign). Pass to the R of a barn, then head up to a ladder-stile into the wood. Go straight through the wood (broad path) to leave it at a stile. ③ Keep straight on, with a fence on the L. When the fence curves L keep straight ahead (aiming towards a distant gasholder). At the wall turn L to a stile in the corner. ④ Stay near the wall on the R to reach a gate and stile into a drive. Go L along it. ⑤ Turn L up the tarmac lane. ⑥ The tarmac ends at the farm, but keep straight on through a gate and up the clear track for 1½ miles to emerge onto the motor road at Nick O' Pendle. ⑦ Turn L. ⑧ Just over the brow of the hill take a gate on the L (FP sign), but before doing so you may fancy nipping down the road to the Wellsprings Inn (¼ mile). Stagger back to the gate and follow the path down to the wall. Turn R alongside it and pass through a gate and stile to follow a sunken track down to the farm buildings at Wymondhouses. ⑨ The official right-of-way goes through the gate, crosses the farmyard, squeezes through a gap between the LH side of a modern barn and a wall, then continues straight on across the field to reach a fence stile near a stream in a wooded clough.

An unofficial diversion (and the farmer would prefer you to go this way) avoids the farmyard by climbing ½ L, passing round the top of a fence to a step stile at the wall corner. Over it, follow the LH field boundary which eventually leads down to the aforementioned stile in the clough. ⑩ Cross the stream to a clear path bearing R up the bank. It soon peters out, but continue in the same direction across a big field to the farm. ⑪ Go through the farmyard and along the farm road. Turn L to follow the lane back to Wiswell. CROSS HIGHER UP

WISWELL is a tranquil, sleepy sort of place, with some affluent-looking houses and some attractively renovated old cottages. It was not always so quiet; in 1870 Wiswell was populated by 465 good souls, many of whom found employment either at the quarries on Wiswell Moor or the mill at nearby Barrow. WISWELL HALL FARM stands on the site of a Tudor house which was the birthplace of John Paslew, last Abbot of Whalley. In 1536 Paslew became involved in a protest (known as the Pilgrimage of Grace) against the suppression of the monasteries. He was subsequently brought for trial at Lancaster on a charge of treason, and sentenced to be hung, drawn and quartered. His bodily remains were then displayed on a gibbet at Whalley. The SHAY (or Shey) CROSS, also known as the 'Weeping Cross', is a restored shaft in an ancient socket. It marks what was a halting place for funeral processions bound for Whalley churchyard.

Shay Cross

WYMONDHOUSES

> THE FIRST CONGREGATIONAL CHURCH IN NORTH EAST LANCASHIRE WAS FOUNDED HERE BY THOMAS JOLLIE IN 1667

When, in the days of religious persecution, the fiery and controversial Rev. Thomas Jollie, Minister of Altham, was expelled from his church, he held secret services for those non-conformists who cared to join him at remote Wymondhouses. The 17th C. farmhouse carries a commemorative plaque above its door.

• • •

Cold Coats Farm has a window from Whalley Abbey in its gable end, and decorated masonry from the Abbey in its walls.

O.S. PATHFINDER (1:25 000) MAP
Nº 680 (SD 63/73) Longridge and Great Harwood)

© Jack Keighley 1992

ROUGHLEE & THE WATER MEETINGS

5¾ MILES

A walk through typical Pendle Forest countryside – a blend of undulating meadowland and open moor. From Roughlee, a village notable for its 'witchly' associations, there is a long, steady climb to Jackson's House, a remote farm standing at over 1000' on lonely Burn Moor. Enjoyment of this satisfying ramble is enhanced by a final 1½ miles of delightful riverside walking.

Water Meetings

NOTE: This is a rather complex route. Easy to go astray. Careful reference to map and directions required.

ROUTE DIRECTIONS

① Walk along Foreside towards main road. Turn R into narrow ginnel (by entrance to Brook Dell Ho.) Follow wall on R up to stile in corner. ② Climb diagonally R to gap at corner of hawthorns, then turn L and cross field to stile in hedge. Keep straight ahead through line of stiles, crossing two farm roads and depression, then up clear path to stile at top L of field. ③ Turn R up lane. In 150 yds take waymarked stile on L. In a few yards turn R through gap in hedge and follow hedge on R up to buildings. ④ Straight on through waymarked stile by gate to climb with hedge on L. When hedge ends keep straight on. When Roughlee appears head for last house on R. Cross stepping stones and turn L to visit village centre. ⑤ Returning from Bay Horse take first lane L and immediately turn R. Pass in front of Hall and L up farm road. Through farmyard and turn R past a house to gate and stile into enclosed green track. ⑥ When hollies on L end turn L across field to gate. Follow wall on R, cross it at a stile, then continue up by wall to stile in corner. As soon as you enter wood bear R and climb diagonally to stile in wall corner (just above level of house) ⑦ Follow wall past house. At wall corner turn L to stile. Cross stile in fence angle and descend LH side of young plantation to footbridge. Up through gap in hollies and head for house. ⑧ Just before reaching house turn L to gate. Use stile to R of farmhouse ahead and go up tarmac drive. ⑨ Turn R along lane and in 30 yds L through gate and up farm road. ⑩ Use two gates to pass to L of farm (yellow marker arrows) then continue uphill alongside wall on R. ⑪ Near modern barn turn R on farm track. Cross cattle-grid. ⑫ Before reaching farm look for stile near wall corner on R. Descend to stile marked with white-topped posts. Keep L in next field to gate in fence, then descend to pass between buildings and down the access road. ⑬ Cross cattle-grid and turn R, off farm road, to locate stile just below gate in fence on L. Aim for big house to find next stile at bottom of field, then cross stile to R of house to reach stream. Don't cross bridge. Turn R and follow stream to a lane. ⑭ Follow L side of stream to another lane. ⑮ Turn R along lane. ⑯ Immediately past farm entrance take stile on L. Go forward with a wall and then a fence on the

A corner of Higherford

Map labels

Burn Moor
⑫
⑪ barn
Jackson's House (farm)
Burn Moor End
barn
farm road
Higher Wheathead ⑩
N
Lower Admergill
⑬
FB
Admergill Water
farm road
⑨
lane
Lower Wheathead
Lanefield
⑧
lane
DON'T go down the farm track here
⑭
FB
⑦
Bank End
⑮
Bank End is a very des. res.
⑯
Blacko Foot
Blacko Water
lane
Pendle Water
WATER MEETINGS
⑰
FB
Old Oak Tree Cottage weir
Hollin Farm
Hall
farm lanes
Bay Horse Inn
⑤
ROUGHLEE
stepping stones (15 cylindrical concrete blocks)
holly hedge
West Pasture lane
④ ③
s/s
chimney
⑦ ② ①
HIGHERFORD

L. When fence ends keep straight on to stile and down to footbridge. Follow stream down to another bridge. ⟨17⟩ Immediately across bridge turn L onto riverside path.

Roughlee Old Hall

In the days when King Cotton ruled the region, ROUGHLEE was a popular Sunday afternoon venue for mill-workers out from the nearby grimy towns in search of some greenery and a breath of fresh air. Nowadays the crowds which flock to Roughlee are of a more heterogeneous nature, for the little village is a favourite haunt of walkers, cyclists, anglers, caravanners, campers and picnickers. The dominant building is the OLD HALL, a late-17th.C house now divided into cottages and much-altered, though still retaining some fine arch-headed mullion windows. Often referred to as 'WITCHES' HALL', it is by repute the one-time home of ALICE NUTTER, one of the Pendle 'witches' who was hanged at Lancaster. It is more likely that she actually lived in a nearby, and now demolished, farmhouse. The severely eroded inscribed stone (THIS HOUSE WAS BUILDED BY MN IN THE YEAR OF OUR LORD 1536) set into the modernized west wing of the Hall originally belonged to the old farm. MN was Miles Nutter, whose son Richard was Alice's husband.

The PACKHORSE BRIDGE off Foreside, Higherford, dates from 1583 ● WEST PASTURE and LOWER WHEATHEAD are 17th.C. farmsteads ● WATER MEETINGS was another popular picnic place for the mill-workers of bygone days. Here the plump little dipper, with its conspicuous white 'bib', can often be seen bobbing and bowing on the boulders. This bird can walk on the river bed.

O.S. PATHFINDER (1:25 000) MAPS
Nº 670 (SD 84/94) Barnoldswick and Earby
Nº 681 (SD 83/93) Burnley

WALKS IN LANCASHIRE WITCH COUNTRY

22

A VISIT TO BRACEWELL

6½ MILES

Lying amidst the soft emerald countryside at the far northern corner of the Borough of Pendle is the hamlet of Bracewell. Though but a tiny cluster of farms and cottages, it is steeped in history and has one of the most beautiful churches in the area. This gently undulating walk from Gisburn is a joy from start to finish.

Bracewell Church J Keighley

ROUTE DIRECTIONS

① From village centre walk along A682 Nelson road and turn R up school drive. At top of drive turn L into narrow field, cross fence stile and follow LH field boundary up to stile in crossfence. ② Straight on towards Pendle Hill. Cross farm road via two small gates and a ditch via stiles and footbridge to reach stile in cross-fence. Straight on past solitary tree to stile in crosswall, then head for building to find stile in far RH corner. ③ Turn R along lane and L into Eel Beck Farm drive, but before reaching house take gate on L. Forward past house, R over footbridge and L to follow stream to stile. ④ Turn R up into caravan park and L along its main drive to exit. ⑤ Turn R along lane and in 100yds take stile on L (FPsign). Keep straight on to gate into main road. Turn R. ⑥ Turn L into Todber Caravan Park. Straight through yard and up past R of house, then bear R through gap in fence and cross corner of field to stile. Climb to fence stile on skyline. ⑦ Over hill, keeping just to R of highest point, and descend to come alongside hedge on R. Cross farm track and straight on through gate and line of stiles. ⑧ Cross rough lane and follow farm road. At farm gate fork L up stony track. ⑨ Take stile on R (PW sign) and forward on LH side of hedge. Pass to R of reservoir. ⑩ Follow PW signs to cross fence up on R, then follow it forward. ⑪ Re-cross fence and keep R of fenced woodland, then descend slightly L to wall stile. Pass L of tennis court to gate into drive. Turn L to road. ⑫ Turn L along road, and L again into farm road (FP Gisburn). Keep R (straight on) at fork, and follow farm road past reservoir. ⑬ 30yds past cattle-grid take stile on R, cross footbridge and bear slightly L up to wall stile. Follow overgrown path up through wood to stile. ⑭ Maintain direction over hill, passing

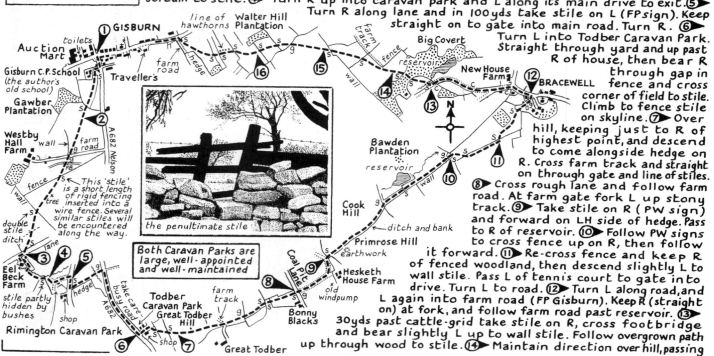

This 'stile' is a short length of rigid fencing inserted into a wire fence. Several similar stiles will be encountered along the way.

the penultimate stile

Both Caravan Parks are large, well-appointed and well-maintained.

GISBURN ① toilets

Auction Mart

Gisburn C.P. School (the author's old school)

Travellers

farm road

Gawber Plantation

Westby Hall Farm wall farm road

fence

tree

double stile
ditch

lane

Eel Beck Farm ③ ④ ⑤

stile partly hidden by bushes

hedge

shop

Rimington Caravan Park

Todber Caravan Park
Great Todber Hill

shop ⑦

⑥

Great Todber

Bonny Blacks

farm track

A682 busy road

take care

Coal Pit Lane ⑨

⑧

old windpump

Hesketh House Farm

Primrose Hill

earthwork

ditch and bank

Cook Hill

reservoir

wall

Bawden Plantation

⑩

⑪

N

New House Farm ⑫ BRACEWELL

⑬

⑭

reservoir

Big Covert

farm track

fence

wall

line of hawthorns

Walter Hill Plantation

hedge

farm road

⑯

⑮

A682 Nelson

②

to L of fence corner and down to stile in crosswall. Make for far LH corner of next field. ⑮▸ Maintain direction, aiming towards wood. Go through small gate and keep below wood to its LH end. ⑯▸ When Gisburn appears head slightly to L of it, through line of stiles, then bear R down sunken track and descend to bottom of farm road. Turn L along main road into Gisburn.

FOR NOTES ON GISBURN SEE WALK 30

ꞙhe GISBURN WITCH
Jennet Preston was one of those arrested for being at the Good Friday 'witches' gathering' at Malkin Tower. She was subsequently charged with causing the death, by charms and sorcery, of Thomas Lister of Westby Hall. As Gisburn was, in those days, in Yorkshire, she was sent for trial not to Lancaster but to York. Evidence was given that after Lister's death she was brought to the house and made to touch the body, which thereupon began to bleed. Only the touch of a murderer, it was stated, could cause a corpse to bleed. She was found guilty, and hanged on 29 July 1612 (3 weeks before the Lancaster hangings).

the 'solitary tree'

The PRIMROSE HILL EARTHWORK, a slightly raised area about 10yds square and barely discernible, is thought to mark the site of a Roman signal tower.

BRACEWELL The small church dates back to Norman times and was originally a private chapel of the Tempest family. An archway from their manor house (demolished 1656) has been re-erected in the churchyard. Nearby, to the SW of the church, is a large barn known as 'King Henry's Parlour', for Henry VI was reputedly given sanctuary there by the Tempests as he fled from the Battle of Hexham in 1464.

south door Bracewell Church

O.S. PATHFINDER (1:25 000) MAP Nº 670 (SD 84/94) Barnoldswick and Earby

© Jack Keighley 1992

WALKS IN LANCASHIRE WITCH COUNTRY

23

THE ASCENT OF PENDLE HILL

FROM WORSTON VIA MEARLEY CLOUGH

7 MILES

One of the most exhilarating walks available in the area, Mearley Clough being perhaps the most dramatic of the many fine ravines which gash the slopes of Pendle. It is also the most strenuous walk in this book, involving almost 1500' of climbing with one unremittingly steep section of some 700'. Not recommended in severe wintry conditions.

Little Mearley Hall

JKeighley

① Walk out of village along Downham road, and at first L bend (Worston Hall is just round corner on L) turn R (FP sign) and go between buildings to gate/stile. ② Follow wall/hedge on L and keep straight on up field to stile just to R of tree. Bear slightly R up next field to small gate, then follow LH side of fence. ③ Turn R along farm road and follow it L up to farm. ④ Straight through farmyard to metal gate R of silage tank and up broad path through trees. Keep between wall on L and stream on R. ⑤ When wall ends follow stream for about 100yds then bear L to climb steep slope. As gradient eases a tall, well-built cairn comes into view. ⑥ From cairn follow cairned path (NE) along rim of escarpment, over stile in crosswall and bear R to follow clear path (E) across moor to gate in wall. ⑦ Go down by near side of wall to step-stile. Return up far side of wall to gate and turn L (SSW) to reach O.S. column at summit. Return to cross step-stile and follow path leading directly away from it. Path runs along hillside before swinging R to descend steeply. Head for RH end of distant plantation. ⑧ Go L along road for just over ¼ mile then turn L up farm road. ⑨ At farm keep straight on through metal gate L of all buildings. Follow wall on R to stile, then bear slightly L (maintain height) to gate. ⑩ Forward along cart track. Just before next gate turn L and go up L of house to a stile. Turn R, through gate and L along farm road. ⑪ Turn L through metal gate set at angle and up clear path to farm. Go through farmyard and along concrete road. ⑫ Cross cattle-grid and turn R. ⑬ When road bends R take field gate on L and descend to gate at bottom of field. ⑭ Turn R, then L in front of house, then L again round modern

PARKING   At Worston, just off the A59(T). The large car park belongs to the pub, and if you wish to use it you *must* seek and obtain permission. Otherwise, parking is difficult, but you may find the odd roadside space. Be sure not to obstruct gates/drives or cause inconvenience to residents. Map ref (Calf's Head Hotel) 768 427

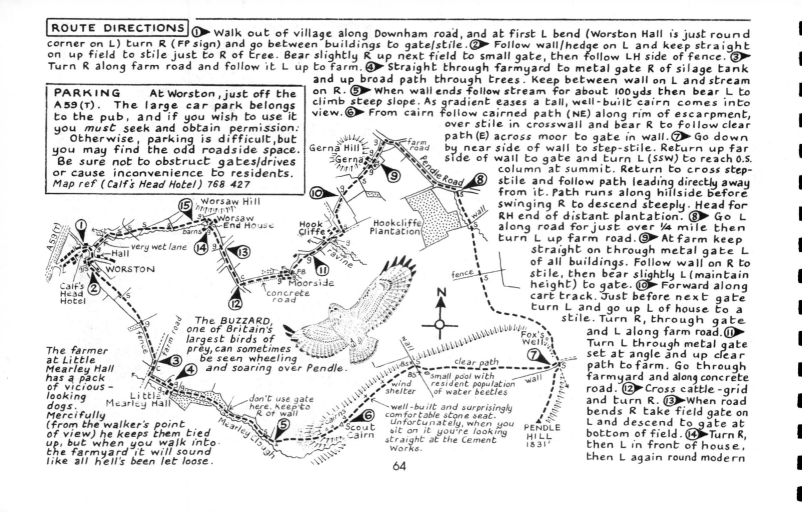

The BUZZARD, one of Britain's largest birds of prey, can sometimes be seen wheeling and soaring over Pendle.

The farmer at Little Mearley Hall has a pack of vicious-looking dogs. Mercifully (from the walker's point of view) he keeps them tied up, but when you walk into the farmyard it will sound like all hell's been let loose.

small pool with resident population of water beetles

well-built and surprisingly comfortable stone seat. Unfortunately, when you sit on it you're looking straight at the Cement Works.

barn to gate. ⑮ Follow stream on L. Look for two ladder-stiles on R, then straight on through slit-stile. Turn L into muddy lane back to Worston.

NOTE that the path up Mearley Clough is not an official right-of-way, though it is provided with a stile and has been regularly used by ramblers for many years.

Crow Hill Cottage, Worston, showing the 'witches' window.

WORSTON claims a

place in local 'witchlore', and it is possible that Demdike's ancestors had some connection with the village. The cottage opposite the Calf's Head Hotel has a small circular window known as 'the witches' window.' The cottage is very old, and, when a fireplace was being altered, clay effigies into which pins had been stuck were discovered, which suggests that witchcraft was once practised here. Worston Old Hall was dismantled c 1800 and the present, smaller house was built with the old stone. The three shields on the porch came from Salley Abbey.

LITTLE MEARLEY HALL is a noble 16th C. house in a lovely, wooded setting.

GEORGE FOX, founder of the Quakers, climbed Pendle in 1652, and afterwards wrote, 'I was moved of the Lord to go up to the top of it, which I did with much ado, as it was so very steep and high. When I was come to the top of this hill I saw the sea bordering upon Lancashire; and from the top of this hill the Lord let me see in what places He had a great people to be gathered. As I went down I found a spring of water in the side of the hill, with which I refreshed myself.'
   You can do likewise, for the well now has an iron lid, beneath which is a cup suspended on a chain.

O.S. PATHFINDER (1 : 25 000) MAPS
            Nº 669 (SD 64/74) Clitheroe and Chipping
            Nº 670 (SD 84/94) Barnoldswick and Earby

WALKS IN LANCASHIRE WITCH COUNTRY

24

READ HEIGHTS

6¼ MILES

   The lower Sabden Valley is bounded on its south side by a low, wooded ridge known as Read Heights. The walk here described meanders through a region steeped in history and endowed with great scenic beauty. It is exceptionally lovely in late Spring and early Summer, when bluebells and rhododendrons adorn the woods and the hillsides blaze yellow with gorse.

footbridge, Sabden Brook

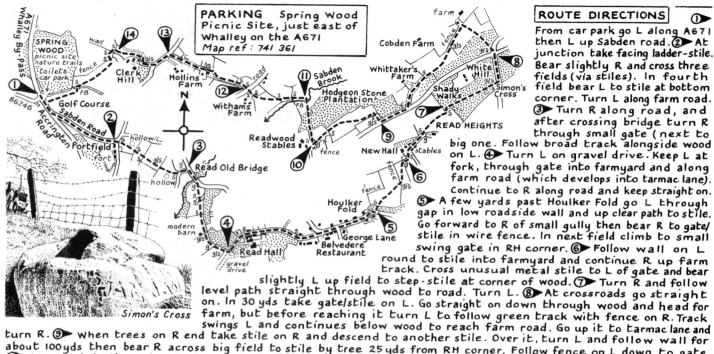

PARKING   Spring Wood
Picnic Site, just east of
Whalley on the A671
Map ref: 741 361

ROUTE DIRECTIONS ①

From car park go L along A671 then L up Sabden road. ② At junction take facing ladder-stile. Bear slightly R and cross three fields (via stiles). In fourth field bear L to stile at bottom corner. Turn L along farm road. ③ Turn R along road, and after crossing bridge turn R through small gate (next to big one. Follow broad track alongside wood on L. ④ Turn L on gravel drive. Keep L at fork, through gate into farmyard and along farm road (which develops into tarmac lane). Continue to R along road and keep straight on. ⑤ A few yards past Houlker Fold go L through gap in low roadside wall and up clear path to stile. Go forward to R of small gully then bear R to gate/stile in wire fence. In next field climb to small swing gate in RH corner. ⑥ Follow wall on L round to stile into farmyard and continue R up farm track. Cross unusual metal stile to L of gate and bear slightly L up field to step-stile at corner of wood. ⑦ Turn R and follow level path straight through wood to road. Turn L. ⑧ At crossroads go straight on. In 30 yds take gate/stile on L. Go straight on down through wood and head for farm, but before reaching it turn L to follow green track with fence on R. Track swings L and continues below wood to reach farm road. Go up it to tarmac lane and turn R. ⑨ When trees on R end take stile on R and descend to another stile. Over it, turn L and follow wall for about 100yds then bear R across big field to stile by tree 25yds from RH corner. Follow fence on L down to gate. ⑩ Immediately through gate turn R to wooden stile and descend sunken path with wall on L. When wall turns L bear slightly R and follow path descending through wood (ignore paths rising to R). Continue down to footbridge. ⑪ Cross bridge and turn L to partially hidden stile (by a tree about 50yds above brook). Straight on to ladder-stile, then bear R up towards farm barn. Just to R of farm, behind a boggy recess in the field corner, is a stile, but it's easier to use gate on R. Go up to stile onto road. ⑫ Take facing stile and climb by small stream on L to farm. Go through gate immediately to R of farmhouse and continue along farm road. ⑬ Turn L along lane and in 200yds turn R into tarmac drive. Just before reaching gate into private grounds take stile on R. Immediately turn L to follow garden fence and perimeter wall to stile in corner. ⑭ Go over wall stile on L and keep L to cross fence stile. Follow fence down, but when it bears R head L across field to stile and slab bridge onto golf course. Descend alongside edge of wood to main road.

SPRING WOOD  A popular picnic site with well-marked nature trails. The wood is especially beautiful in May when the bluebells flower. In winter flocks of long-tailed tits can often be seen.	Behind the farm buildings at PORTFIELD are some remains of an Iron Age hill fort which occupied the site of an even earlier Bronze Age settlement. Permission to visit must be obtained from the house called 'Llamedos'. The large barn by the roadside was a tithe barn built by the monks of Whalley Abbey.

READ OLD BRIDGE was the site of a Civil War skirmish in April 1643. Here an army of Lancashire Royalists was ambushed and routed by a small band of local Roundheads.

READ HALL was the home of Roger Nowell J.P., the magistrate who was responsible for bringing the Pendle witches to trial in 1612. The Nowell estate was sold in 1772 to the Fort family, who built the present Regency-style mansion between 1818 and 1835.

The deep, overgrown trench alongside the path in SHADY WALKS was a drift mine for the extraction of fire clay. The pedestal of SIMON'S CROSS, which marked the boundary separating Read and Simonstone, is locally known as 'Wart Well', for the water which collects in its socket is said to cure warts.

Shady Walks

O.S. PATHFINDER (1:25 000) MAP
Nº 680 (SD 63/73) Longridge and Great Harwood

© Jack Keighley 1992

67

WALKS IN LANCASHIRE WITCH COUNTRY

25

WHITE MOOR & ADMERGILL WATER

7¼ MILES

This stimulating walk, on the fringe of Pendle Forest, reaches a height of just over 1100' without involving any steep climbing. The route encircles 'Blacko Tower', which, next to Pendle itself, is the most outstanding landmark in the area. The terrain is delightfully varied, with rolling pastures giving way to bleak moorland and, finally, the delectable little valley of Admergill Water.

Admergill Hall

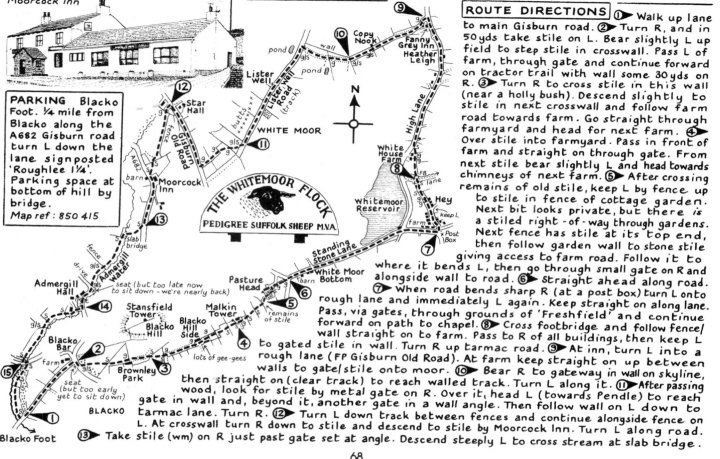

① Walk up lane to main Gisburn road. ② Turn R, and in 50 yds take stile on L. Bear slightly L up field to step stile in crosswall. Pass L of farm, through gate and continue forward on tractor trail with wall some 30 yds on R. ③ Turn R to cross stile in this wall (near a holly bush). Descend slightly to stile in next crosswall and follow farm road towards farm. Go straight through farmyard and head for next farm. ④ Over stile into farmyard. Pass in front of farm and straight on through gate. From next stile bear slightly L and head towards chimneys of next farm. ⑤ After crossing remains of old stile, keep L by fence up to stile in fence of cottage garden. Next bit looks private, but there is a stiled right-of-way through gardens. Next fence has stile at its top end, then follow garden wall to stone stile giving access to farm road. Follow it to where it bends L, then go through small gate on R and alongside wall to road. ⑥ Straight ahead along road. ⑦ When road bends sharp R (at a post box) turn L onto rough lane and immediately L again. Keep straight on along lane. Pass, via gates, through grounds of 'Freshfield' and continue forward on path to chapel. ⑧ Cross footbridge and follow fence/ wall straight on to farm. Pass to R of all buildings, then keep L to gated stile in wall. Turn R up tarmac road. ⑨ At inn, turn L into a rough lane (FP Gisburn Old Road). At farm keep straight on up between walls to gate/stile onto moor. ⑩ Bear R to gateway in wall on skyline, then straight on (clear track) to reach walled track. Turn L along it. ⑪ After passing wood, look for stile by metal gate on R. Over it, head L (towards Pendle) to reach gate in wall and, beyond it, another gate in a wall angle. Then follow wall on L down to tarmac lane. Turn R. ⑫ Turn L down track between fences and continue alongside fence on L. At crosswall turn R down to stile and descend to stile by Moorcock Inn. Turn L along road. ⑬ Take stile (wm) on R just past gate set at angle. Descend steeply L to cross stream at slab bridge.

PARKING Blacko Foot. ¼ mile from Blacko along the A682 Gisburn road turn L down the lane signposted 'Roughlee 1¼'. Parking space at bottom of hill by bridge.
Map ref: 850 415

THE WHITEMOOR FLOCK
PEDIGREE SUFFOLK SHEEP M.V.A.

Moorcock Inn

Follow riverside path downstream to pass in front of Admergill Hall. ⑭▶ Turn R over bridge, then keep L of house and round far end of it to stile. Continue along riverside path .⑮▶ At road bridge, riverside path transfers to L side of stream.

> There is NO RIGHT-OF-WAY up to Blacko Tower. Permission to visit must be sought at Tower Farm, reached from the Gisburn road about half-a-mile north of Blacko Bar.

MALKIN TOWER FARM IS BELIEVED BY SOME TO BE THE SITE OF MALKIN TOWER, HOME OF OLD MOTHER DEMDIKE, BUT THERE IS NO REAL EVIDENCE TO SUPPORT THIS THEORY. IT WAS MORE PROBABLY NEAR NEWCHURCH (see Walk 9)

BLACKO TOWER or *Stansfield Tower, or Jonathan's Folly, was built by Jonathan Stansfield, a local grocer, in 1890. It was restored in 1950.*

The tiny MOUNT PLEASANT METHODIST CHAPEL (point ⑧) was founded by Rev. John Barritt, an early follower of John Wesley, in 1822. Outside steps lead to the first floor chapel.

The FANNY GREY INN is named after a horse. If you want to know the story, call in and ask the land-lord. And whilst you're in there, treat yourself to one of his excellent bar lunches.

—•—●—•—

ADMERGILL HALL, a splendid early 17th.C. building in a delightful setting, stands by an ancient packhorse route linking Colne and Whalley. Note nearby the old 'clam' or slab bridge. Over the centuries a deep groove has been worn along its length by the passage of countless feet and hooves.

> O.S. PATHFINDER (1 : 25 000) MAP
> Nº 670 (SD 84/94) Barnoldswick and Earby

© Jack Keighley 1992

26

WHALLEY & THE NAB

5¾ MILES

Whalley is renowned for its Abbey and quite superb Parish Church. 'Whalley and The Nab' is a convenient title, but the walk extends well to the south of The Nab, crossing the pleasantly wooded Dean Valley to reach the outskirts of Great Harwood. There are fine views – particularly of Pendle Hill and across to the Bowland Fells.

Whalley Church

PARKING At Whalley. Car park in village centre, behind the Whalley Arms. Map ref : 734 362

The heraldic shields in Whalley Church's unusual and beautiful east window include the arms of several local families who were involved in the 'Witch Trials' of 1612.

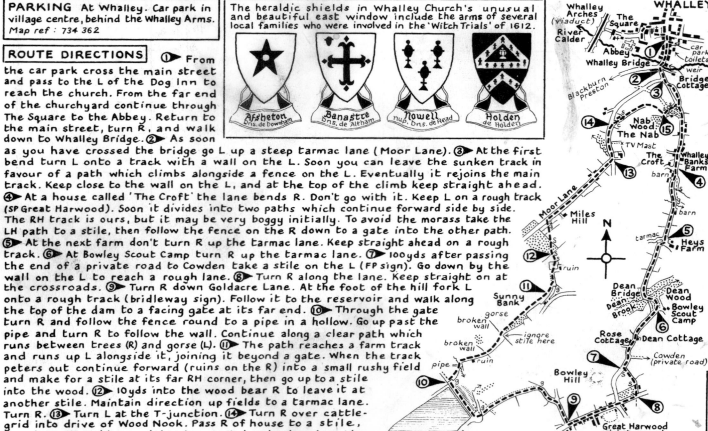

ROUTE DIRECTIONS

① From the car park cross the main street and pass to the L of the Dog Inn to reach the church. From the far end of the churchyard continue through The Square to the Abbey. Return to the main street, turn R, and walk down to Whalley Bridge. ② As soon as you have crossed the bridge go L up a steep tarmac lane (Moor Lane). ③ At the first bend turn L onto a track with a wall on the L. Soon you can leave the sunken track in favour of a path which climbs alongside a fence on the L. Eventually it rejoins the main track. Keep close to the wall on the L, and at the top of the climb keep straight ahead. ④ At a house called 'The Croft' the lane bends R. Don't go with it. Keep L on a rough track (SP Great Harwood). Soon it divides into two paths which continue forward side by side. The RH track is ours, but it may be very boggy initially. To avoid the morass take the LH path to a stile, then follow the fence on the R down to a gate into the other path. ⑤ At the next farm don't turn R up the tarmac lane. Keep straight ahead on a rough track. ⑥ At Bowley Scout Camp turn R up the tarmac lane. ⑦ 100yds after passing the end of a private road to Cowden take a stile on the L (FP sign). Go down by the wall on the L to reach a rough lane. ⑧ Turn R along the lane. Keep straight on at the crossroads. ⑨ Turn R down Goldacre Lane. At the foot of the hill fork L onto a rough track (bridleway sign). Follow it to the reservoir and walk along the top of the dam to a facing gate at its far end. ⑩ Through the gate turn R and follow the fence round to a pipe in a hollow. Go up past the pipe and turn R to follow the wall. Continue along a clear path which runs between trees (R) and gorse (L). ⑪ The path reaches a farm track and runs up L alongside it, joining it beyond a gate. When the track peters out continue forward (ruins on the R) into a small rushy field and make for a stile at its far RH corner, then go up to a stile into the wood. ⑫ 10yds into the wood bear R to leave it at another stile. Maintain direction up fields to a tarmac lane. Turn R. ⑬ Turn L at the T-junction. ⑭ Turn R over cattle-grid into drive of Wood Nook. Pass R of house to a stile, then keep straight on, with a low, walled embankment on the

70

R. when the embankment ends bear slightly R towards a Nissen hut seen through the trees. ⑮ ▶ On reaching a fence turn L and descend to a stile. Cross the farm road and keep on down, with a fence on the L, to rejoin the outward route.

WHALLEY

Twinned with
VIHIERS
FRANCE

This large village has sufficient charm and historical interest to attract thousands of visitors a year. THE SQUARE is the old village centre, and most of its buildings date from the 17th. C., but in addition to these Whalley has many lovely old cottages and fine Tudor and Georgian houses. But Whalley's pride and joy is undoubtedly THE PARISH CHURCH OF ST. MARY AND ALL SAINTS – once the Mother Church for half of Lancashire. An excellent guidebook is available, and its 26 pages are crammed with information on the wealth of treasures to be seen in and around a truly outstanding church with a history spanning 13 centuries.

In 1288 a small company of Cistercian monks came to Whalley from Stanlow Abbey in Cheshire to found a new monastery. They met with many difficulties, and it was not until 1308 that the foundation stone was laid. The early parts of the Abbey were built of golden-brown gritstone quarried on Whalley Nab. The Abbey took 127 years to build and became one of the most powerful in the North of England. There are two very fine gateways; the West Gate is backed rather incongruously by the red-brick railway viaduct known as Whalley Arches (built 1850). The grounds and ruins are open daily from 10 a.m. (1 p.m. on Sundays).

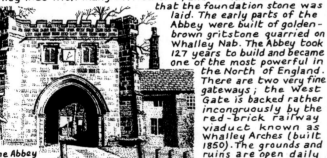

The Abbey N.E. Gate

• Bridge Cottage, near Whalley Bridge, is where Harrison Ainsworth wrote his famous novel 'The Lancashire Witches' (1848).

O.S. PATHFINDER (1: 25 000) MAP
Nº 680 (SD 63/73) Longridge and Great Harwood
© Jack Keighley 1992

27

THE ASCENT OF BOULSWORTH HILL

FROM TRAWDEN

6¼ MILES

This is quite a strenuous walk, and one for which clear weather is essential. The North West Water Authority's concessionary footpath allows access to the top of Boulsworth, which, with its clusters of bizarre gritstone outcrops, is a grand place to be on the right kind of day. The view from the summit is superb in all directions.

the summit of Boulsworth Hill

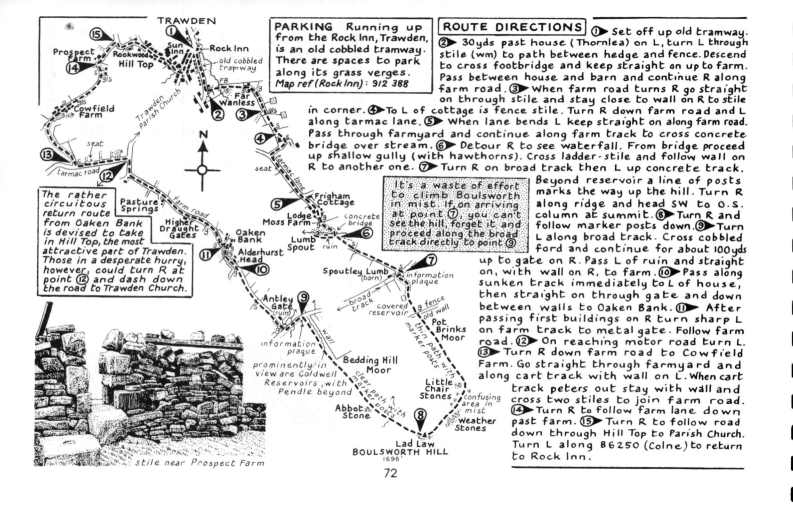

TRAWDEN

Map labels: Prospect Farm (15), Rookwood Hill Top (14), Sun Inn (1), Rock Inn, old cobbled tramway, Cowfield Farm, Trawden Parish Church, Far Wanless (2)(3), seat, (13) tarmac road, (12), Pasture Springs, Higher Draught Gates, Frigham Cottage, seat, tarmac lane, Lodge Moss Farm, concrete bridge, Oaken Bank (11), Alderhurst Head (10), Lumb Spout, ruin, (6), (7), Spoutley Lumb (barn), information plaque, Antley Gate (9) (ruin), broad track, covered reservoir, thin path with marker posts, old wall, fence, Pot Brinks Moor, information plaque, wall, Bedding Hill Moor, clear path with marker posts, Little Chair Stones, confusing area in mist, Abbot Stone, (8), Weather Stones, Lad Law BOULSWORTH HILL 1696, N

PARKING Running up from the Rock Inn, Trawden, is an old cobbled tramway. There are spaces to park along its grass verges. Map ref (Rock Inn): 912 388

The rather circuitous return route from Oaken Bank is devised to take in Hill Top, the most attractive part of Trawden. Those in a desperate hurry, however, could turn R at point (12) and dash down the road to Trawden Church.

It's a waste of effort to climb Boulsworth in mist. If, on arriving at point (7) you can't see the hill, forget it and proceed along the broad track directly to point (9).

prominently in view are Coldwell Reservoirs, with Pendle beyond

stile near Prospect Farm

ROUTE DIRECTIONS

(1) Set off up old tramway. (2) 30yds past house (Thornlea) on L, turn L through stile (wm) to path between hedge and fence. Descend to cross footbridge and keep straight on up to farm. Pass between house and barn and continue R along farm road. (3) When farm road turns R go straight on through stile and stay close to wall on R to stile in corner. (4) To L of cottage is fence stile. Turn R down farm road and L along tarmac lane. (5) When lane bends L keep straight on along farm road. Pass through farmyard and continue along farm track to cross concrete bridge over stream. (6) Detour R to see waterfall. From bridge proceed up shallow gully (with hawthorns). Cross ladder-stile and follow wall on R to another one. (7) Turn R on broad track then L up concrete track. Beyond reservoir a line of posts marks the way up the hill. Turn R along ridge and head SW to O.S. column at summit. (8) Turn R and follow marker posts down. (9) Turn L along broad track. Cross cobbled ford and continue for about 100yds up to gate on R. Pass L of ruin and straight on, with wall on R, to farm. (10) Pass along sunken track immediately to L of house, then straight on through gate and down between walls to Oaken Bank. (11) After passing first buildings on R turn sharp L on farm track to metal gate. Follow farm road. (12) On reaching motor road turn L. (13) Turn R down farm road to Cowfield Farm. Go straight through farmyard and along cart track with wall on L. When cart track peters out stay with wall and cross two stiles to join farm road. (14) Turn R to follow farm lane down past farm. (15) Turn R to follow road down through Hill Top to Parish Church. Turn L along B6250 (Colne) to return to Rock Inn.

TRAWDEN

In Norman times the Forest of Trawden was a vast hunting ground. During the 13th and 14th centuries monastic cattle farms, or 'vaccaries', were established, and some developed into small settlements such as Trawden, Winewall and Wycoller. Trawden's growth into a large village was stimulated by the arrival of the textile industry. Most of Trawden's oldest buildings, however, are to be found clustered in delightfully haphazard fashion in the HILL TOP area. The village features quite prominently in Lancashire 'witchlore'. It was whilst bound for Trawden that Alizon Device met and, allegedly, bewitched a peddlar at Colne – an incident which 'triggered-off' the great witch-hunt of 1612. Stories of witchcraft were also rife in Trawden in the mid-19th. century.

Trawden's first tram arrived at the ROCK INN (the original terminus) on 22.6.1904. As the village street beyond that point was too narrow to accommodate trams, a special extension TRAMWAY was built. This was opened on 21.12.05. The last tram left Trawden on 3.6.28.

FAR WANLESS is an attractive and well-maintained 17th.C house.

—•—•—•—

LUMB SPOUT is a slender waterfall set in a lovely wooded hollow. In its heyday as a beauty spot there was a bungalow and café here – the ruins can be seen just above the waterfall.

—•—•—•—

OAKEN BANK is the tiniest of hamlets, but there was a time when more than 100 people lived here, many of whom were hand-loom weavers. The first buildings on the right show how a row of cottages (18th C) has been converted into stables.

Abbot Stone

O.S. PATHFINDER (1 : 25 000) MAP
Nº 681 (SD 83/93) Burnley

© Jack Keighley 1992

73

28

KELBROOK MOOR

7 MILES

This invigorating West Craven ramble provides absolutely outstanding views from a succession of splendid vantage points. It's a grand place to be – especially in spring, when the upland pastures resound with the exultant song of the skylark and the wild, haunting call of the curlew. In late summer, too, the walk is a joy, for then the moors are ablaze with heather.

summit of
Knarrs Hill

PARKING At Kelbrook, 2½ miles N of Colne on the A56. Space to park a few cars in the vicinity of the church. Map ref: 903 448

ROUTE DIRECTIONS

① From church go along Harden Road, turn R over stone bridge then L to follow lane alongside beck. ② Just past Dotcliffe Mill turn L up narrow lane. At cattle-grid take stile on R and turn R uphill on far side of wall. Turn L at line of trees and follow them to gate. ③ Turn R and follow hedge on R through two fields to stile in corner, then straight across next field to stile by gate. Turn L along farm road. ④ Straight through farmyard, over stile in fence and maintain direction through two fields, then bear R up to house. ⑤ Go down lane past house and over small footbridge on R. Clear path slants R up hillside (just below line of poles) to stile. Pass to L of derelict farm and follow wall on R to stile in corner. ⑥ Diagonally L across next field to ladder-stile at its top LH corner. Follow wall down to Black Lane Ends. ⑦ Turn L up road and in a few yards R along lane. ⑧ Turn R into farm road (wm and sign - Knarr End Farm). Stay with it as it rounds a small plantation then heads R across fields. When it turns L towards farm keep straight on up to O.S. column. ⑨ Cross stile and follow wall on L down to stile. Descend L to farm, over stile into farmyard, pass to R of house and along farm road. When road forks keep R down to next house. ⑩ Turn R over stile by gate. Keep R of all buildings to gate. Straight on to another gate then bear R to next farm. ⑪ Turn L down farm road. Immediately after first house turn R through small gate and go straight up field to steps down to road. ⑫ Turn L along road. Just past Hawthorn Cottage turn R up farm road. Pass L of farm and on up stony farm road. ⑬ Turn L in front of next farm into walled track. When wall on L ends, turn R through old iron gate onto open moor. Cross moor, keeping just to R of trees, then descend gradually to stile by gate in crosswall. ⑭ Head forward alongside wall on L, but when it begins to descend towards farm keep straight on, maintaining height, to reach

SHORT CUT

If you're a bit weary, or pushed for time (having spent too long in the Hare and Hounds), you could turn R at Black Lane Ends and proceed by road to point ⑫ (½ mile). The walk would then be reduced to 5 miles.

see note on SHORT CUT

The farm road from point ⑧ is less than ¼ of a mile from the Yorkshire border.

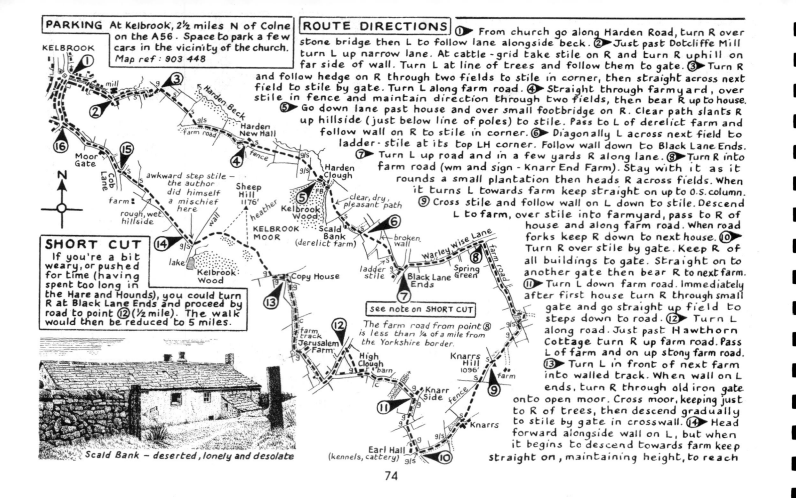

Scald Bank - deserted, lonely and desolate

KELBROOK
KELBROOK MOOR
Harden Beck
Harden New Hall
Harden Clough
Harden farm road
Moor Gate
Cob Lane
awkward step stile - the author did himself a mischief here
Sheep Hill 1176'
rough, wet hillside
farm
Kelbrook Wood
Scald Bank (derelict farm)
lake
Kelbrook Wood
Copy House
broken wall
ladder stile
Black Lane Ends
Warley Wise Lane
Spring Green
farm road
farm track
Jerusalem Farm
High Clough
barn
Knarrs Hill 1096'
farm
Knarr Side
fence
Knarrs
Earl Hall
(kennels, cattery)

a ladder-stile. Descend by ruined wall to stile. ⑮▶ Turn L out of farm road and R down lane. ⑯▶ At bottom of Cob Lane turn R back to church.

KELBROOK

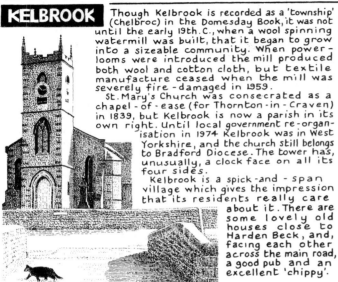

Though Kelbrook is recorded as a 'township' (Chelbroc) in the Domesday Book, it was not until the early 19th.C., when a wool spinning watermill was built, that it began to grow into a sizeable community. When power-looms were introduced the mill produced both wool and cotton cloth, but textile manufacture ceased when the mill was severely fire-damaged in 1959.

St. Mary's Church was consecrated as a chapel-of-ease (for Thornton-in-Craven) in 1839, but Kelbrook is now a parish in its own right. Until local government re-organisation in 1974 Kelbrook was in West Yorkshire, and the church still belongs to Bradford Diocese. The tower has, unusually, a clock face on all its four sides.

Kelbrook is a spick-and-span village which gives the impression that its residents really care about it. There are some lovely old houses close to Harden Beck and, facing each other across the main road, a good pub and an excellent 'chippy'.

In bygone days BLACK LANE ENDS had a pub, a school and a Methodist chapel. Only the pub – the Hare and Hounds – now remains in business. This cosy, friendly hostelry dispenses Timothy Taylor's ale, the finest in the North (in the author's opinion). ● From the trees between points ⑬ and ⑭ the O.S. column on SHEEP HILL, the highest point of the moor, can be seen away to the right. A visit to this fine viewpoint entails but a simple detour – but note there is no official right-of-way.

O.S. PATHFINDER (1:25 000) MAP
Nº 670 (SD 84/94) Barnoldswick and Earby

© Jack Keighley 1992

29

AROUND THE WITCH'S POLE

4¾ MILES

The 'Witch's Pole' is a local name for Stang Top Moor, one of Pendle's eastern foothills. The walk begins in sylvan surroundings, following a sparkling stream down its wooded valley from Barley to White Hough, before heading north to encounter a much more open and bleak landscape. Some interesting old buildings are seen on this easy ramble over gently undulating terrain.

J. Keighley

Higher Black Moss Farm

cottage at Over Houses

PARKING At Barley. There is a car park and information centre at the south end of the village, off the Nelson road. (During winter the information centre opens only at weekends).
Map ref : 823 403

ROUTE DIRECTIONS

①► Go to the east end of the car park (towards the mill chimney), where a waymarked path leads out onto a narrow tarmac lane. Go L along it, passing between the cottages of Narrowgates to continue alongside the stream. **②►** Just before reaching the buildings of White Hough take a stile (with a small gate) on the L. Go up through a gate, then turn R to follow the lane between the buildings. Keep straight on up a walled tarmac lane. **③►** At the far side of a small red-brick building a stile gives access to a wood. Keep close to the LH edge of the wood to cross two plank bridges. After the second bear slightly L to reach a stile at the edge of the wood. Go up towards the farm. **④►** Before you get to the farm cross a fence stile (between hollies) on the L and turn R across the field to a waymarked stile. Follow the fence forward. At the end of the field turn R over a stile, descend to the farm road and turn L. **⑤►** Turn L up the tarmac lane then R over a cattle-grid and along Hollin Top farm road. **⑥►** As soon as the road becomes fenced on the R, turn L and climb the hillside to a holly at the end of a wall. Turn R on a broad track which contours round the hillside. **⑦►** When the track forks keep R to descend to a cottage. Turn L here and go up, with a wall on the L, to a fence stile. Follow the fence R to a wall. Descend by the wall to a stile at the bottom of the field. **⑧►** In the next field keep R up to the farm. Immediately past the farm go through a gap by a small gate and turn L to follow the wall. **⑨►** Turn L along the tarmac lane. In 60yds take a step stile on the R and bear ½ L to cross another step stile. Turn R and follow the field boundary round to a farm. **⑩►** Use a gate on the R to pass to the R of all the buildings and continue forward to the next farm. **⑪►** Bear ½ L, aiming towards Pendle's highest point. Join a wall coming in from the R and continue alongside it. **⑫►** Go R down the tarmac lane. Turn L through a gate (footpath sign) and follow the wall on the L before deflecting R to a gate. Continue between wall and stream to enter a walled lane. **⑬►** Pass through the farmyard and turn R to a small waymarked gate. Keep L across the field to a stile in the corner then follow the clear path, passing through two swing gates and on down to Over Houses. **⑭►** For a short detour to see Darney's

Cottage go through the field gate to the L of the white house. Return to cross the bridge and turn R through a small gate (SP Barley). Follow the streamside path down to a walled lane. ⑮ Turn R along the lane and then L through the village.

● The isolated chimney at NARROWGATES belonged to a water-powered cotton mill which was built by William Hartley c 1800. The mill closed down in 1967, the oldest parts then being demolished and the rest converted into a private house. The mill pond was filled in to make the visitors' car park. Our walk passes between the rows of former weavers' cottages.
● WHITE HOUGH has a long history, for it is known that a vaccary (cow farm) existed here in the 13th C. The Grange was built in 1593. The nearby Camp School was founded in 1938.
● SALT PIE owes its odd name to the fact that a pile (pie) of salt used to be maintained here for the general use of local people - mainly for food preservation.
● UPPER BLACK MOSS RESERVOIR (12¾ acres - 31'deep) dates from 1894. The lower reservoir (17¾ acres - 41'deep) was completed in 1903. They provide drinking water for Nelson.

Darney's Cottage
This ancient house, with its arch-headed mullion windows, dates from c1580. William Darney, a cobbler and preacher, came south with Bonny Prince Charlie and lived here from about 1746 to his death in 1774. A contemporary of John Wesley, Darney helped to form the Methodist movement.

DON'T ENTER the building. It is unsafe.

O.S. PATHFINDER (1:25 000) MAP
Nº 670 (SD 84/94) Barnoldswick and Earby

30

GISBURNE PARK & PAYTHORNE
5¾ MILES

A leisurely stroll through magnificent parkland into that beautiful part of Craven where the Ribble swings westwards into Lancashire and where the salmon come to spawn. On a sunny Autumn day, when the scenery at Gisburn Bridge in particular is an absolute riot of red and gold, this is a walk to uplift the soul.

JKeighley

caravans
g/s
8
9 g/s F8 + ex school
Loftrans Farm
Hewitts Farm barn
S F8
PAYTHORNE
10 g.r. S
S
S hedge
Moor House Farm g
big barn
Paythorne Bridge
11
7
N
g/s
Castle Haugh g fence
Windy Pike Farm
splendid 17thC farmhouse
6
g/s
MS
River Ribble
Carter's Lane g
BS
12
tumulus
Ellenthorpe (kennels)
13
5
A682
hospital
Gisburn Bridge c
Stock Beck
2
Coppice wood
3 4 GISBURNE PARK
Deer House Farm (farm shop, picnic area)

The strange, turreted building near the river at Gisburn Bridge is an old sawmill.

Mill Lane
industrial estate
Auction Mart
tunnel
1
Travellers
GISBURN

ROUTE DIRECTIONS

Parish Church of St. Mary the Virgin, Gisburn

① Walk to west end of village and turn R along Bolton-by-Bowland road. ② Just before reaching Gisburn Bridge turn R to go up narrow, leafy tarmac lane behind buildings. ③ Keep R at junction of lanes to cross cattle-grid, then keep L (straight on) along tarmac drive. ④ Cross main hospital drive to go down track between fence and wall. Cross bridge and follow main track as it swings L and climbs to gate at edge of wood. Continue along cart track. ⑤ Turn L along road. ⑥ Turn L over stile (bridleway and RW signs), then turn R and head for RH end of line of trees. Pass, via two gates, to R of mound and ditch, then follow fence on R down to gate into wood. Clear path descends through wood to Paythorne Bridge. ⑦ Cross bridge and follow road up to Paythorne. ⑧ At far side of Buck Inn turn L (SP Windy Pike) to gate/stile. Head for far RH corner of field, where you cross small stream and, a few yards further on, a stile on R. Keep well to L of caravan site, and aim for distant farm buildings to locate footbridge. ⑨ Bear R to climb far bank, then L to cross field (keep parallel with the fence some 80 yds to the R) to reach wooden stile. Continue forward by line of hawthorns to stile, then straight on over another stile to a metal gate. ⑩ Continue forward alongside hedge on L, then bear slightly R to gates into farmyard. Pass through farmyard, keeping to R of big barn. ⑪ After passing this barn, fork L along farm road. Keep L of next farm to continue L down farm road. ⑫ After crossing cattle-grid turn L along tarmac lane. ⑬ Turn L at next road-junction (Gisburn I) and follow road down to Gisburn Bridge. Continue along road back to Gisburn.

GISBURN HAD ITS OWN INDIGENOUS WITCH – SEE WALK 22

GISBURN

GISBURN is a quaint and charming village. Peaceful, however, it is not, for it is rent asunder by the incessant stream of vehicles roaring and thundering along the A 59. The ancient and beautiful church has a 13th C porch and 14th C tower, and its lovely stained glass includes medieval fragments. The village retains some 17th C buildings and has three splendid inns. An inscription on the porch of the Ribblesdale Arms informs us that

New Inn and Ribblesdale Arms, Gisburn

it was built in 1635, and bears the name of Thomas Lister. The Listers were Lords of Ribblesdale, and their estates stretched from Clitheroe to Malham. They lived at Westby Hall (see Walk 22) from the 14th C to the late 1700s, when Gisburne Park (a Georgian mansion now a private hospital) became their family seat. 'Gisburne' is the old spelling – the village dropped the 'e' in the late 19th C.

CASTLE HAUGH, a huge mound encircled by a dry ditch, is almost certainly the site of an early Norman motte and bailey castle. On the mound would have stood a wooden keep.

PAYTHORNE, an ancient Domesday manor, is best known for its 'Salmon Sunday' (the Sunday nearest to November 20th), when crowds gather to watch the fish coming up to their spawning beds in the gravelly shallows above Paythorne Bridge. The Buck Inn is a popular pub. The tiny Methodist Church was built in 1830

Windy Pike Farm

O.S. PATHFINDER (1:25 000) MAPS
Nº 670 (SD 84/94) Barnoldswick and Earby
Nº 661 (SD 85/95) Skipton and Hellifield

© Jack Keighley 1992

79

PLEASE OBSERVE THE
COUNTRY CODE

- Enjoy the countryside and respect its life and work

- Use gates and stiles to cross walls and fences

- Keep your dog under close control

- Protect wildlife, plants and trees

- Help to keep all water clean

- Make no unnecessary noise

- Fasten all gates

- Leave livestock, crops and machinery alone

- Keep to public paths across farmland

- Take special care on country roads

- Guard against all risk of fire

- Leave no litter

LITTER

NOTES

From ghoulies and ghosties and long leggety beasties,
And things that go bump in the night,
Good Lord deliver us.
Amen